HOW CAN ONE
NOT BE INTERESTED IN

Belgian History

WAR, LANGUAGE AND CONSENSUS
IN BELGIUM SINCE 1830

First edition: September 2005
Second edition: March 2006
Third edition: December 2006
Fourth edition: June 2007

© Academia Press
Eekhout 2
9000 Gent
Belgium
Tel. + 32 9 233 80 88 – Fax +32 9 233 14 09
info@academiapress.be – www.academiapress.be

The publications of Academia Press are distributed by:

J. Story-Scientia bvba Scientific Booksellers
Sint-Kwintensberg 87
9000 Gent
Belgium
Tel. +32 9 225 57 57 – Fax +32 9 233 14 09
info@story.be – www.story.be

Ef & Ef
Eind 36
6017 BH Thorn
The Netherlands
Tel. +31 475 561 501 – Fax +31 475 561 660

How Can One Not Be Interested in Belgian History
War, language and consensus in Belgium since 1830
Gent, Academia Press, 2005, 152 p.

ISBN 978 90 382 0816 9
D/2005/4804/142
NUR1 688
NUR2 694
U 763

HOW CAN ONE *NOT* BE INTERESTED IN

Belgian History

WAR, LANGUAGE AND CONSENSUS
IN BELGIUM SINCE 1830

BENNO BARNARD / MARTINE VAN BERLO
GEERT VAN ISTENDAEL / TONY JUDT
MARC REYNEBEAU / SOPHIE DE SCHAEPDRIJVER

WITH A FOREWORD BY THE BELGIAN & DUTCH
AMBASSADORS IN DUBLIN, IRELAND

A CO-EDITION OF TRINITY COLLEGE DUBLIN
& ACADEMIA PRESS, GENT

WILFRIED GEENS and JACOBUS VAN DER VELDEN

Ambassador of Belgium and Ambassador of the Netherlands in Dublin

———

Foreword

This little volume is the outcome of a symposium *Belgium Revealed*, held on April 8, 2005, at Trinity College, Dublin.

It was organised on the initiative of Martine Van Berlo, lecturer in Netherlands languages at Trinity, under the aegis of the Department of Germanic Studies of the College, in close co-operation with the embassies of Belgium and the Netherlands in Dublin.

Before a substantial audience, four prominent authors from Belgium and the Netherlands each highlighted a specific (mostly critical) vision of the origins of Belgium's independence and of what that complex notion of 'belgitude' is ultimately all about.

The rebellion of 1830 against the Kingdom of the Netherlands was led by a small group of citizens from the Francophone upper middle classes, somewhat indistinctly underpinned by popular discontent. Belgian independence, from the view of historians today, was almost an accident, rather than the inevitable consummation of pent-up nationalism. Had it not been for the political stubbornness of King William, the United Kingdom of the Netherlands might well have survived and become a thriving economic giant encapsulated in a strong middle-sized state.

The audience heard that Belgian culture is shaped by deep-seated traditions of local autonomy, leading to a certain provincialism of the upper classes, and to what one author calls *petit bourgeois* anarchism'. Most Belgians are rather weary of strong state authority. But the suspicion towards state authority has always gone hand in hand with a strong sense of individual tolerance. Provincial pragmatism became the foundation for a kind of solidarity based on a continuous search for consensus and a refusal of violent confrontation.

Belgium is a European natural. The coexistence of several languages overlapping the borders of a small national territory provided political and corporate leaders with natural skills of inter-cultural and international dialogue. The transition from nation-state to European partner was a remarkably smooth one in Belgium. Belgians possess a 'lasagne' sense of identity: they are attached to a city, a region, a country and – why not – a European Union.

The Irish public, quite used to its own history of confrontation with a powerful neighbour, seemed impressed by the pragmatic and easy way with which the young Belgian nation-state was able to interact with its previous French and Dutch occupants. Europe's old-time favourite battlefield turned into a natural meeting ground between the north and south of the continent.

Members of the Irish public seemed quite astonished by the paradox of some very critical and irreverent observations about Belgium on the one hand, coupled on the other hand with great attachment to the existence of the country and its role on the international stage.

One of the challenges was explaining how this small nation's recovery of its freedom became an inspiration and a *leitmotiv* for the aspirations of many other European peoples to national independence and individual freedoms – the Irish people among them.

Irish listeners were intrigued to hear that the notorious opposition between Flemish and Francophone only became an issue in the early part of the twentieth century ... that this division coincided with social class divisions at a time when social advancement presupposed adoption of the French language ... and that the overall history of Belgium cannot be viewed simply through the linguistic prism since both language groups were and are largely heterogeneous.

An unexpected image of Belgium was projected for our Irish friends of a post-nationalist, federal country, combining cultural pragmatism with a rather solid social consensus ... A country quite capable of playing its own role on the European and international scene.

———

With these few lines and comments, may we express our appreciation and gratitude to the four speakers, Marc Reynebeau, Geert van Istendael, Benno Barnard and Professor Sophie de Schaepdrijver. Our thanks also to the moderators Professors Horne, Comerford and Downey and to Mario Danneels. Special thanks are due to the driving force behind the event, Trinity's Lektorin for Dutch and Low Countries Studies, Martine Van Berlo.

MARTINE VAN BERLO, LIC.PHIL.,

PROF. DR. MORAY MCGOWAN,

DR. TIM JACKSON, TRINITY COLLEGE DUBLIN

Belgium in the Department of Germanic Studies, TCD

D utch language and culture have an important place in the work of the Department of Germanic Studies at Trinity College Dublin. On April 8, 2005, with the financial and logistical support of the Belgian and Dutch embassies, a symposium entitled *Belgium Revealed* was organised to celebrate Belgium's 175th birthday and 25 years of Belgian Federalism. We would like to thank everybody who made this event such a great success and made this publication possible.

Thanks too to the students of Dutch for the inspiration they have given us through their awakening interest in Belgian history and culture. Our biggest debt of gratitude goes to the two embassies and their ambassadors, HE Wilfried Geens and HE Jacobus Van der Velden, whose help and support inspired us to develop the idea of the symposium. Our thanks also to Olivier Quinaux, Bert van der Lingen, Lieve Broodcoorens and Xuan Tran for their invaluable assistance.

We would like to thank Academia Press, especially Dr. Geert Van den Bossche, for their expert advice and editorial support, and particularly our panellists and those other colleagues who generously found time to chair their sessions: Professor John Horne of the Department of Modern History, TCD, Professor Vincent Comerford of the Department of Modern History, NUI Maynooth, Dr. Declan Downey of the Department of Modern History, UCD and Mario Danneels, Dublin correspondent of *De Standaard*.

If you were a member of the large audience at this event, we hope this little book will help you remember it; if you were not, we hope it will give you a flavour of the wit, stimulation and thought-provoking qualities our four speakers brought to their talks and the lively and wide-ranging panel discussions. Their critical engagement with Belgium was much more than that: it was a day of engagement with big questions about Europe and the future of nations. We thank them profusely.

TONY JUDT

Is There A Belgium? *

Brief initiation to Belgian life and to this country's history

Belgium gets a bad press. A small country – the size of Wales, with a population of just ten million – it rarely attracts foreign notice; when it does, the sentiment it arouses is usually scorn, sometimes distaste. Charles Baudelaire, who lived there briefly in the 1860s, devoted considerable splenetic attention to the country. His ruminations on Belgium and its people occupy 152 pages of the *Oeuvres Complètes*; Belgium, he concluded, is what France might have become had it been left in the hands of the bourgeoisie.[1] Karl Marx, writing in a different key, dismissed Belgium as a paradise for capitalists. Many other exiles and émigrés have passed through the country; few have had much good to say of it.

I am neither an exile nor an émigré, but I too had the occasion recently to spend an extended period in Belgium. Unlike most temporary visitors to the country, however, I was not in Brussels, but in a small Flemish village not far from Bruges; and in contrast to most of Belgium's transitory foreign residents today I could claim at least a slender bond to the place since my father was born there, in Antwerp. Daily life in rural Flanders is uneventful, to say the least; it is only with time that you become aware of the uneasy, troubled soul of this little corner of the European Union. Belgium has much to commend it beyond the self-deprecatingly touted virtues of beer and waffles; but its salient quality today may be the illustration that this small country can furnish of the perils now facing states everywhere.

You do not have to be there for very long to be reminded that during the last decade of the twentieth century Belgium has been a cornucopia of scandals. The latest of these, mass poisoning of the local food chain through the leakage of dioxin (a highly toxic substance) into chicken feed and pig swill, briefly emptied the village supermarkets – though English-speaking visitors were firmly assured that the health risks were negligible compared to those associated with British beef or genetically engineered American corn. But before dioxin Belgium had had other scandals: money laundering, graft and kickbacks in high places, political assassin-ations, kidnapping, paedophilia, child murder, police incompetence, and wholesale administrative corruption.

All of this has happened in a tiny, prosperous region of northwest Europe whose national capital is also the headquarters of 'Europe' (whose bureaucracies are largely segregated from Belgium in an unsightly glass and concrete ghetto). But half the population of the country – the Dutch-speaking Flemings – have divided and federalised it to the point of near extinction, while the French-speaking other half has no distinctive iden-tity. Not surprisingly, there have been suggestions that Belgium might do better just to melt away. Would it matter? Who would care? [2]

Whether Belgium needs to exist is a vexed question, but its existence is more than a historical accident. The country was born in 1830 with the support of the Great Powers of the time – France, Prussia, and Britain, among others – none of whom wished to see it fall under the others' sway.

The territory it occupies had been (and would remain) the cockpit of European history. Caesar's *Gallia Belgica* lay athwart the line that would separate Gallo-Roman territories from the Franks. When Charlemagne's empire fell apart in the ninth century, the strategically located 'Middle Kingdom' – between the lands that would later become France and Germany – emerged as a coveted territorial objective for the next millennium. The Valois kings, Bourbons, Habsburgs (Spanish and Austrian), Napoleon, Dutch, Prussian Germans, and, most recently, Hitler have all invaded Belgium and claimed parts of it for themselves, occupying and ruling it in some cases for centuries at a time. There are probably more battlefields, battle sites, and reminders of ancient and modern wars in Belgium than in any comparably sized territory in the world.

Belgians, then, could be forgiven for a degree of uncertainty about their national identity. The state that came into being at the London Conference was removed from the control of the Dutch, furnished with a newly minted king from Germany, a constitution modelled on the French one of 1791, and a new name. Although the term 'Belgium' had older roots (the twelfth-century chronicler Jean de Guise attributed it to a legendary monarch, *Belgus*, of Trojan provenance), most of the inhabitants of the region identified only with their local community. Indeed, urban or communal loyalty lay at the core of whatever was distinctive about the place. From the thirteenth century onward, Flemish towns had come together to fight off the fiscal and territorial claims of lords, kings, and emperors. Even today Belgium is the only country in Europe where identification with the immediate locality trumps regional or national affiliation in the popular imagination.

The new Belgian state rested on a highly restricted suffrage that confined power and influence to the French-speaking nobility and commercial and industrial bourgeoisie; in practice it was held together not by any common feeling of Belgianness but by hierarchically organised social groups – 'pillars' (*piliers* in French, *zuilen* in Dutch) – that substituted for the nation-state. Catholics and anticlericals in particular formed distinct and antagonistic communities, represented by Catholic and Liberal political parties. These parties, in turn, served not just to win elections and control the state but to mobilise and channel the energies and resources of their 'pillar'. In each case an electoral constituency doubled as a closed social, economic, and cultural community.

With the emergence in the 1880s of a Socialist party that sought to control the growing industrial working class, the 'pillarisation' of Belgium into Liberal, Catholic, and Socialist 'families' was complete. From the late nineteenth century until very recently, Belgian public and private life has been organised around these three distinct families – with antagonism between Socialists and Catholics steadily displacing in significance the older one between Catholics and Liberals. Much of daily life was arranged within hermetically separated and all-embracing nations-within-a-nation, including child care, schooling, youth groups, cafés, trade unions, holiday camps, women's groups, consumer cooperatives, insurance, savings societies, banking, and newspapers.

At election time, especially following the expansion of the suffrage (extended to all men in 1919, to women in 1948), governments could only be formed by painfully drawn-out coalition building among the parties representing these pillars. Such coalitions were typically unstable (there were eighteen governments between the world wars and there have been thirty-seven since 1945). Meanwhile political, judicial, civil service, police, and even military appointments are made by 'proportionality', which is to say that they are assigned to clients and friends within the pillars through a complex and corrupting system of agreements and deals.

Some of this story is of course familiar from other countries. The 'culture wars' of Imperial Germany and the parliamentary instability of Fourth Republic France come to mind, as does the *proporz* system of public appointments in Austria today and the clientele-driven venality of post-war Italy (two countries likewise born in uncomfortable and contested circumstances). But Belgium has two distinguishing features. First, the pervasive system of patronage, which begins in village councils and reaches to the apex of the state, has reduced political parties largely to vehicles for the distribution of personal favours. In a small country where everyone knows someone in a position to do something for them, the notion of an autonomous, dispassionate, neutral state barely exists. As Belgium's current prime minister, Guy Verhofstadt, said in the mid-eighties, Belgium is little more than a party kleptocracy.

The language conflict:
two interconnected yet so different cultures

S econd: below, above, within, and across the social organisations and political divisions of Belgian society runs the yawning fault line of language. In the northern half of the country (Flanders, Antwerp, Limburg, and much of Brabant, the region around Brussels), Dutch is spoken; in the southern half ('Wallonia', which stretches from Hainaut in the west to Luxembourg in the east), French. Living in the village of Zedelgem, close to the much-travelled tourist sites of Bruges and Ghent and just twenty minutes from the frontier with French-speaking Hainaut, I encountered many Dutch speakers who cannot (or will not) speak French; a much larger proportion of the French-speaking population of the country has no knowledge of Dutch. Brussels, officially 'bilingual', is predominantly French-speaking, but in essence a multicultural enclave within the Dutch-speaking sector. Today these divisions are immutable, and they correspond quite closely to an ancient line dividing communities that fell respectively under Romanic or Germanic rule.[3]

Their origins, however, are fairly recent. French, the court language of the Habsburg monarchy, became the language of the administrative and cultural elite of Flanders and Wallonia during Austrian rule in the eighteenth century. This process was reinforced by the French revolutionary occupants and their Napoleonic heirs. Meanwhile the peasants of Flanders continued to speak (though less frequently read or write) a range of local Flemish dialects. Despite a shared language base, Flemings and Dutch were divided by religion; the Flemish Catholics' suspicion of the Protestant ambitions of the Dutch monarchy contributed to their initial welcome for an independent Belgian state. Domination by French speakers was reinforced by early-nineteenth-century industrialisation; impoverished Flemish peasants flocked to Wallonia, the heartland of Belgium's wealth in coal and steel. It is not by chance that many French-speaking Walloons today have Flemish names.

The Belgian state was Francophone, but French was not imposed – the 1831 constitution (Article 23) stated, in effect, that Belgian citizens could use the language of their choice. French was required only for government business and the law. But when a movement for Flemish-language rights and a distinctive Flemish identity began to assert itself in the mid-nineteenth century, it had little difficulty demonstrating that in practice Dutch speakers, or the speakers of regional Flemish dialects, were at an acute disadvantage in their new state. They could not be tried in their own language; secondary and higher education was *de facto* a Francophone near monopoly; and French-speaking interests looked after themselves at the expense of their Flemish co-citizens. When American grain imports began to undercut and destroy the home market for Flemish farmers, the Brussels government refused to establish protective tariffs for fear of retribution against (Walloon) industrial exports.

The conflation of linguistic rights and regional interests was thus present from the outset in Flemish resentment of 'French' domination. Once a suffrage reform in 1893 gave the vote to a growing body of Dutch-speaking citizens from the north, most of whom were solidly organised within the Catholic social and political 'pillar', the state was forced to compromise with their demands. By 1913, Dutch was officially approved for use in Flemish schools, courts, and local government. In 1932, a crucial step was taken, when Dutch became not just permitted but required in Flemish schools. The union of language and region – the creation of two administratively distinct unilingual territories conjoined only by the overlap in Brussels – was now inevitable.

This process, implicit in the language legislation between the two world wars, was delayed by World War II. As in World War I, Flemish radicals tried to take advantage of the German occupation of Belgium to advance the separatist cause. On both occasions, German defeat set them back. After World War II in particular the memory of the wartime collaboration of the ultra-separatist *Vlaams Nationaal Verbond* (VNV) discredited the Flemish case for a generation. At the same time, the postwar punishment of collaborators rankled, as did the abdication of King Leopold III in 1950. The King's ambivalent behaviour during the war had discredited him with many Belgians, but a referendum in March 1950 produced a national vote of 58 percent in favour of keeping him (among Dutch-speaking voters, 72 percent voted for the King). However, demonstrations in Wallonia and Brussels, where a majority wanted to see Leopold go, forced him to step aside in favour of his son Baudouin, leaving many Flemings resentful of the way the vote, and their preference, had been overturned. [4]

What finally doomed the unity of Belgium, however, was the reversal of economic fortunes. Where once French-speaking Wallonia had dominated, it was now in precipitous decline. During the fifties 200,000 jobs were lost as the mines of the Sambre-Meuse region closed. Coal mining, steel making, glass, slate and metallurgical industries, textile production – the traditional core of Belgian industrial power – virtually disappeared. In 1961 twenty-one million tons were still produced; now all Belgian coal mines are closed. Only the residue of what was once the continent's most profitable industrial conurbation remains, in the decrepit mills of the Meuse valleys above Liège and the gaunt, silent mining installations around Mons.

The country that built the first railway in continental Europe (from Brussels to Malines), and that still has the densest rail network in the developed world, now has little to show for it but an unemployment rate, in Wallonia, among the highest in Western Europe. In Charleroi and the neglected industrial villages to its west, middle-aged men gather listlessly in dingy, decaying cafés; they and their families owe their subsistence to Belgium's generous and vigorously defended welfare system, but they are doomed to a superannuated existence of extended, involuntary retirement and they know it.

Flanders, meanwhile, has boomed. Unencumbered by old industry or an unemployable workforce, towns like Antwerp and Ghent have flourished with the growth of service technology and commerce, aided by their location at the heart of Europe's 'golden banana', running from Milan to the North Sea. In 1947 over 20 percent of the Flemish workforce was still in agriculture; today fewer than 3 percent of Dutch-speaking Belgians derive their income from the land. There are more Dutch speakers than French speakers in the country (by a proportion of three to two), and they produce and earn more per capita. This process, whereby the Belgian north has overtaken the south as the privileged, dominant region, has been gathering speed since the late fifties – accompanied by a crescendo of demands from the Flemish for political gains to match their newfound economic dominance.

The complex and confusing political structure

The demands of the Flemish for political gains have been met. Through several revisions of the constitution in just thirty years, the Belgian unitary state has been picked apart and reconstructed as a federal system. The results are complex in the extreme. There are three 'Regions': Flanders, Wallonia, and 'Brussels-Capital', each with its own elected parliament (in addition to the national parliament). Then there are three 'Communities': the Dutch-speaking, the French-speaking, and the German-speaking (representing the approximately 65,000 German speakers who live in eastern Wallonia near the German border). These, too, have their own parliaments. To simplify things, the two Flemish parliaments and their corresponding governments have merged into one parliament and one government. This operation did not take place on the Francophone side.

The regions and the linguistic communities don't exactly correspond – there are German speakers in Wallonia and some French-speaking towns (or rather parts of towns) within Flanders. Special privileges, concessions, and protections have been established for all of these, a continuing source of resentment on all sides. Two of the regions, Flanders and Wallonia, are effectively unilingual, with the exceptions noted. In bilingual Brussels, the 'official' majority of the population speaks French (as testified by the language on their identity card; probably only just over 50 percent speaks French at home).

There are, in addition, ten provinces (five each in Flanders and Wallonia) and these, too, have administrative and governing functions. But real authority lies either with the region (in matters of urbanism, environment, the economy, public works, transport, and external commerce) or the linguistic community (education, language, culture, and some social services). The national state retains responsibility for defence, foreign affairs, social security, income tax, and the (huge) public debt; it also administers the judicial system. But the Flemish are demanding that powers over taxation, social security, and justice shift to the regions. If these are granted, the unitary state will effectively have ceased to exist.

The politics of this constitutional revolution are convoluted and occasionally ugly. On the Flemish side, extreme nationalist and separatist parties have emerged. *Vlaams Belang*, spiritual heir to the VNV, is now the leading party in Antwerp, though, in the City Council, it is relegated to the opposition benches. Up to now, the traditional Dutch-speaking parties refuse to form coalitions with the *Vlaams Belang*. On the other hand, they have been forced (or tempted) to take more sectarian positions. Similarly, in Wallonia and Brussels, politicians from the French-speaking mainstream parties have adopted a harder 'community' line to accommodate Walloons who resent Flemish domination of the political agenda.

All the mainstream parties have split along linguistic and community lines: the Christian-Democrats (since 1968), the Liberals (since 1972), and the Socialists (since 1978) all exist in duplicate, with a Flemish and a Francophone party of each type; up to the 1999 elections, the Christian-Democrats dominated Flemish politics. Today, there is more power sharing in Flanders. The Socialists remain all-powerful in Wallonia, and the Liberals are prominent in Brussels. The result is further deepening of the rift between the communities, as politicians and electors now address only their own 'kind'. [5]

One of the crucial moments in the 'language war' came in the sixties, when Dutch-speaking students at the University of Leuven (Louvain) objected to the presence of French-speaking professors and classes at a university situated within Dutch-speaking *Vlaams-Brabant*. Marching to the slogan of *"Walen buiten!"* ('Walloons Get Out!'), they succeeded in breaking apart the university, whose Francophone members headed south into French-speaking *Brabant-Wallon* and established the University of Louvain-la-Neuve. In due course the university library, too, was divided and its holdings redistributed, to mutual disadvantage.

These events, which occurred between 1966 and 1968 and brought down a government, are still remembered among French speakers – just as many Flemings continue to meet annually on the last Sunday of August in Diksmuide, in West Flanders, to commemorate Flemish soldiers killed in World War I under the command of French-speaking officers whose orders they could not understand. The memorial tower erected there in 1930 carries the inscription "*Alles voor Vlaanderen – Vlaanderen voor Kristus*" ("All for Flanders – Flanders for Christ"). On the Belgian national holiday – July 21, which commemorates Leopold of Saxe-Coburg's ascent to the throne in 1831 as Leopold I of Belgium – flags are still hung out in Wallonia, but I did not see many in the tidy little villages of Flanders. Conversely, the Flemish authorities in 1973 decreed that they would recognise the date of July 11 in celebration of the victory of the Flemish towns over the French king Philippe le Bel at the Battle of the Golden Spurs in 1302. This does not mean, however, that many Flemish flags are seen on that day in Flanders.

The outcome of all this is absurdly cumbersome. Linguistic correctness (and the constitution) now require, for example, that all national governments, whatever their political colour, be 'balanced' between Dutch- and French-speaking ministers, with the prime minister the only one who has to be bilingual (and who is therefore typically a Fleming). Linguistic equality on the Constitutional Court is similarly mandated, with the presidency alternating annually across the language barrier. In Brussels, the four members of the executive of the capital region sit together (and speak in the language of their choice) to decide matters of common concern; but for Flemish or Francophone 'community' affairs they sit separately, two by two. Whenever money in Brussels is spent on 'community' affairs – schools, for example – it must always be apportioned exactly 80:20, in accordance with the officially fixed ratio of the respective language groups. Even the automatic information boards on interregional trains switch to and fro between Dutch and French (or to both, in the case of Brussels) as they cross the regional frontiers.

As a consequence Belgium is no longer one, or even two, states but an uneven quilt of overlapping and duplicating authorities. To form a government is difficult: it requires multi-party deals within and across regions. The political symmetry which used to be required between national, regional, community, provincial, and local party coalitions has been given up recently, but a working majority in both major language groups is still needed. And when a government is formed, it has little initiative: even foreign policy in theory the responsibility of the national government – is effectively in the hands of the regions, since for Belgium it mostly means foreign trade agreements and these are a regional prerogative.

The country today

J ust what remains of Belgium in all this is unclear. Entering the country by road you could be forgiven for overlooking the rather apologetic signpost inscribed with a diminutive "*België*" or "*Belgique*". But you will not miss the colourful placard informing you of the province (Liège, say, or West-Vlaanderen) that you have just entered, much less the information board (in Dutch or French, but not both) indicating that you are in Flanders or Wallonia. It is as though the conventional arrangements had been inverted: the country's international borders are a mere formality, its internal frontiers imposing and very real.

The price that has been paid to mollify the linguistic and regional separatists and federalists is high. In the first place, there is an economic cost; it is not by chance that Belgium has one of the highest ratios of public debt to gross domestic product in Western Europe. It is expensive to duplicate every service, every loan, every grant, every sign. The habit of using public money (including EU regional grants, a rich source of provincial and local favours) on a proportional basis to reward clients of the various pillars has now been adapted to the politics of the language community: ministers, state secretaries, their staffs, their budgets, and their friends are universal, but only in Belgium do they come attached to a linguistic *Doppelgänger*. The 1999 government, top-heavy with carefully balanced representation of every possible political and regional interest, was no exception, illustrating, as one political commentator put it, the "surrealist inflation of portfolios and subdivision of responsibilities." [6]

But the cost of Belgium's peculiar politics goes beyond the charge on public money. Belgian insouciance in the face of urban planning – the gross neglect that has allowed Brussels to become a metaphor for all that can go wrong in a modern city – is not new. Baudelaire in 1865 was already commenting upon the "*tristesse d'une ville sans fleuve*" as the burghers of Brussels buried the local stream under tarmac and cobblestones. But the disastrous 'urban renewal' of the 1960s, and the soulless monumentalism of the 'Europe' district of Brussels today, bear witness to a combination of unrestrained private development and delinquent central authority that is distinctively federal in nature – there is simply no one in charge, even in the capital.

The Dioxin Affair in the Summer of 1999 ("Chickengate" to the delighted editorialists of *Le Monde*) illustrated the same problem. The troubling feature of the scandal was not just that one or more suppliers of animal feed had ignored the usual sanitary precautions and leaked a lethal substance into the food chain. It was also that the government had known about it for weeks before telling either the European Union or its own public; and when the news did come out, the government in Brussels had no idea what to do about it or how to prevent a similar occurrence in the future. The main concern of the Belgian government was how to appease and recompense infuriated farmers for the animals that had to be destroyed and the sales that were lost: many Flemish farmers belong to the *Boerenbond*, a powerful organisation of Flemish agribusiness, which is part of the Catholic 'pillar' of Flemish politics, and was thus a power base of the then Christian-Democratic prime minister, Jean-Luc Dehaene.

In the absence of government oversight the striking incidence of high-level corruption and graft is no surprise (Baudelaire again: "*La Belgique est sans vie, mais non sans corruption*"). Belgium has become sadly notorious as a playground for sophisticated white-collar criminals, in and out of government. At the end of the 1980s, the Belgian government contracted to purchase forty-six military helicopters from the Italian firm Agusta and to give the French company Dassault the job of refitting its F-16 aircraft; competing bidders for the contracts were frozen out. It later emerged that the *Parti Socialiste* (in government at the time) had done very nicely from kickbacks on both deals.

The Dassault/Agusta affair was especially significant not just for the links between government, politics, business, and graft, but because of the apparent involvement of organised crime – something already evident in a number of murders and kidnappings through the eighties and early nineties. These were followed by a series of highly publicised crimes against children, culminating in the truly awful affair of Marc Dutroux.

Dutroux and his accomplices, all based in the depressed industrial towns of southern Wallonia, were responsible between 1993 and 1996 for the kidnapping, rape, or murder of six girls, two of them starved to death in a cellar under Dutroux's house. What stirred the public to anger were not only the crimes but the astonishing incompetence of the police charged with finding the criminals. Belgium's police forces were characteristically many and divided. In the Dutroux Affair they were competitive – each trying to keep a step ahead of the other in the hunt for the abductors of the girls. As a result they actually impeded each other's inquiries. In addition, they were inept. When Dutroux, a convicted rapist on parole, was questioned by police at his home, the house (where the children were hidden and still alive) was never searched.

The scandals and the Belgian society

The horror of the Dutroux affair triggered a deep anger and frustration in the Belgian public; in October 1996 300,000 people marched through Brussels to protest against crime, corruption, incompetence, the heartless and ineffective response of the authorities, and the sacking of an overzealous magistrate thought to be too 'sympathetic' to the victims. In view of the impact of this affair on Belgian society, it is not surprising to learn that the Belgian government has undertaken an elaborate reform of the Belgian police and judicial systems. In 2004 Dutroux was convicted to a life sentence.

The embarrassing dioxin scandal in early 1999 may have had even more lasting consequences. In the elections of June 13, 1999 the Belgian voters finally threw Dehaene's Christian-Democrats out of office for the first time in forty years. The Socialists lost votes everywhere and the Liberals (loosely comparable to Germany's Free Democrats in their business-friendly politics) came into government under Guy Verhofstadt – young (forty-six) by local standards and the first Liberal prime minister since 1884.

Moreover, the Greens (known in Wallonia as *Ecolo* and in Flanders as *Agalev*) entered government for the first time, together with the *Volksunie*, a Flemish nationalist party founded in 1954 but somewhat moderated in tone since then. In the meantime this party has been broken up into three separate groups, one linked to the Social-Democrats, one to the Christian-Democrats and some individual MP's melting into the Liberal party. This breakthrough of such small, non-'pillar' parties, ending the throttlehold on government of the three established groupings, may be a passing reaction to the scandals, a protest vote and nothing more. The same elections also saw an increase in the vote for *Vlaams Belang* in Flanders and Brussels; in the Antwerp districts, where it topped the poll, its rhetoric and even its posters eerily echo Jörg Haider in Austria, Christoph Blocher in Switzerland, and Jean-Marie Le Pen in France. Like them, *Vlaams Belang* uses nationalist rhetoric as a smokescreen for anti-immigrant and racist demagogy, and its growing support does not necessarily correspond to much real interest in its separatist programme. But beyond the protests and the frustration something else is happening.

Belgium today is held together by little more than the King, the public debt – and a gnawing collective sense that things cannot continue as they have. Of course the desire for a political housecleaning, Italian-style, is quite compatible with demands for even more federalisation – as radical Flemish politicians have not failed to point out, both the Agusta and the Dutroux scandals originated in Wallonia. But this argument no longer carries as much weight as it did – and risks the charge of cynical opportunism. The generation of the sixties, now in power, continues to play the federalist and communalist cards; but recent polls suggest that most people, even in Flanders, no longer put regional or language issues at the head of their concerns.

This is especially true of new Belgians: the children of immigrants from Italy, Yugoslavia, Turkey, Morocco, or Algeria have more pressing concerns. Even those who identify strongly with Flanders (or Wallonia) don't see a need to abolish Belgium, much less conjoin their fate to another country, or to 'Europe.' Language politics, then, may have blown themselves out in Belgium – though there is a risk that those who have built political careers on them may be slow to appreciate the change.

For similar reasons, the old 'pillars' are in decline. Younger Belgians see the world rather differently. They are not much moved by appeals to sectoral interest – the same prosperity that has underwritten the 'Flemish miracle' has defanged the politics of linguistic resentment. What is more, Belgians no longer align themselves with a single party or community in every facet of their lives. Declining religious practice, the accessibility of higher education, and the move from countryside to town have weakened Catholic and Socialist parties alike. In their place has come the rise of single-issue, 'à la carte' voting. This is a desirable development – without the 'pillars' Belgian politics and public life may well become more transparent, less cozy and corruption-prone. In short, they will cease to be distinctively Belgian. But what, then, will keep the country together?

One answer is prosperity. The obvious difference between Belgium and other, less fortunate parts of Europe where politicians exploit communal sensibilities and corruption flourishes, is that Belgium is rich. Brussels may be an unappealing, seamy city and unemployment may be high in Wallonia, but life for most people in Belgium is tranquil and materially sufficient. The country is at peace – if not with itself then at least with everyone else. If Belgium disappeared, many Belgians might not even notice. Some observers even hold the country up as a postnational model for the twenty-first century: a virtually stateless society, with a self-governing, bilingual capital city whose multinational workforce services a host of transnational agencies and companies.

Even the transportation system has a curiously decentered, self-deprecating quality. A major junction in the trans-European network, Brussels has three railway stations; but none of them is a terminus – trains to Brussels go to and through all three stations. The 'Central Station' is, symptomatically, the least of them – obscure, featureless, and buried underground beneath a heap of concrete. As with its stations, so with the city itself: Brussels has successfully effaced itself. Whatever was once 'there' has been steadily dismantled. The outcome is an unaspiring anonymity, a sort of underachieving cultural incognito of which Sarajevo and Jerusalem can only dream.

But the scandals and their shadow won't go away. In the 1990s, it seemed to many that the Belgian state could no longer perform its primary mission: the protection of the individual citizen. Swayed by political and economic forces beyond its control, caught between federalist decentralisation and uncoordinated, incompetent government agencies without resources or respect, Belgium is the first advanced country truly at the mercy of globalisation in all its forms. It is beginning to dawn on more than a few Belgians that in progressively dismantling and disabling the unitary state in order to buy off its internal critics, they may have made a Faustian bargain.

As we have entered the twenty-first century, an uncertain era in which employment, security, and the civic and cultural core of nations will all be exposed to unprecedented and unregulated pressures beyond local control, the advantage will surely lie with countries whose governments can offer some guarantees of protection and a sense of cohesion and common purpose compatible with the preservation of civil and political liberties. So Belgium does matter, and not just to Belgians. Far from being a model, it may be a warning: after the twentieth century we all know that you can have too much state. But Belgium may be a useful reminder that you can also have too little.

------

*   This essay first appeared in *The New York Review of Books* 46 (December 2, 1999) 19, 49-53. It is reprinted with the kind permission of its author. Where needed, the text was updated by Geert van Istendael and Marc Reynebeau.

[1] See Charles Baudelaire, *Oeuvres Complètes* (Paris, 1961), 1317-1469.

[2] It is not clear where Belgium would go. In our day neither the Dutch nor the French have shown any interest in acquiring it; anyway, few Flemings or Walloons feel much affinity with their fellow Dutch or French speakers across the border. For Walloons in particular the problem of just who they are is a recurrent theme in their literature; on this and much else about the dilemmas of being Belgian, see Luc Sante's fine book *The Factory of Facts* (New York/London, 1998).

[3] See Astrid von Busekist, *La Belgique: Politique des langues et construction de l'Etat* (Brussels, 1998).

[4] On postwar retribution and its aftermath, see Luc Huyse & Steven Dhondt, *La Répression des collaborations 1942-1952: Un passé toujours présent* (Brussels, 1991).

[5] The main newspapers, *Le Soir* and *De Standaard*, have almost no readers outside the French- and Dutch-speaking communities respectively. As a result, neither takes much trouble to report news from the other half of the country (and when the Flemish press recently reported rumours of a royal 'love child' born to King Albert of a foreign mistress, Francophone commentary treated these as politically motivated slurs upon the sole surviving symbol of Belgian unity). When someone speaks Dutch on Walloon television (and vice versa) subtitles are provided. It is only partly a jest to say that English is now the common language of Belgium.

[6] Jean-Pierre Stroobants, in *Le Soir*, July 13, 1999.

MARTINE VAN BERLO

___

A Belgian Tale
A Family, a Nation, a History

O ne hundred and seventy five years of Belgian independence (1830-2005) and twenty five years of federal Belgium (1980-2005). Against this backdrop my own family's story reveals itself as a very Belgian, but also a very Flemish tale, displaying, so to speak, the colours of the Belgian flag as well as the Flemish one: the tricolour of Brabant, and the Lion of Flanders, with and without red tongue and paws. My family's history mirrors – in a very modest sense, of course – Belgium's history, from the time of my great-great-grandfather down to myself, a history conserved and narrated in family myths stretching from the early nineteenth-century to my birth in the mid-1960s, four years before the first wave of federalisation set in train by the State Reform of 1970. In this one family's story we can see reflected the development from unitary Belgium to the federal state as we know it today.

A Family: Walloon-Flemish Crossings

L et's begin with my Walloon great-grandfather (on my mother's side) who, after moving to Flanders, became a genuine Belgian citizen by founding a family with a Flemish girl.

His name was Victor Larue (1868-1927), and he was born in Warsage, a French-speaking country village in the province of Liège. His mother, Marie Cupers (1838-1900), did indeed have a Flemish name, but my grand-mother asserts that her father only learned 'proper' Dutch when he had to, for his job, and then did so in three months. Initially, in the first decades after Belgian independence it had become customary for government services in Flanders to be staffed by French speakers. Then, after the Equality Law of 1898, the government began looking for bilingual Walloons, and so Victor Larue, with his 'perfect' Dutch learnt in such a short space of time, was sent to Brecht, in the north of the province of Antwerp. In his monolingual French obituary of 1927, he is named as the *"Chef de section de L'Accise"* and *"décoré de la Croix civique de 1ère Classe"*. Our family myth calls him *'chef van d'accijnzen'* (chief tax inspector).

Through his job he got to know his future wife when he was monitoring a distillery belonging to the De Munnynck family next to Bridge 11 in Brecht: my great-grandmother Joanna/Jeanette Meeussen (1878-1946) was the bridgekeeper's daughter. The young couple married and had three daughters: Julia (1903), Martha (1907) and Margaretha (1913), who had noticeably Flemish names, and were born in three different Flemish places: Mechelen, Lier and Brecht. It was my great-grandmother's cousin, pastor Raebroeckx of St. Jan's Church in Mechelen, who – when baptising my grandmother and her two sisters – ensured that they got Flemish first names. The children were brought up bilingually; my grandmother Julia spoke French at home, but she also learned a smattering of English in a French-speaking secondary boarding school in 's Gravenwezel.

After her father's death in 1927 the family moved to his parental home in Warsage. The second sister, Aunt Martha, stayed behind in Lier. She had just gained her primary teacher's diploma, and being genuinely perfectly bilingual she was asked to work as a governess for Baron Zuylen's children, which she did until she married in 1930.

As a young woman Julia lost her heart in French-speaking Warsage. However, pastor Raebroeckx intervened again, insisting that Julia, his goddaughter, marry Jozef, a good Flemish boy from the 'Noorderkempen'. In the charged atmosphere of language repression after the Great War, Raebroeckx himself was punished by Cardinal Mercier, the archbishop of Mechelen, for supporting the Flemish Movement: he was transferred to a poor parish in Boom in the Rupel brickyards area. After Cardinal Mercier's death in 1926, however, Cardinal Van Roey allowed him to return to his parish in Mechelen, where he died in 1945, after having been priest for 53 years.

My grandparents married in 1934 in the Warsage parish church, jointly with my great-aunt Marguerite/Margaretha and her husband Joseph. Their wedding mass was celebrated by the fervently Flemish Raebroeckx, but the local pastor was allowed to conduct the wedding ceremony of Aunt Marguerite and Uncle Joseph in French. Grandma Julia left the Warsage of her dreams, and with it her job in the Visé post office, and followed Jozef, the Flemish farmer and ex-soldier from the First World War whom her godfather had chosen, to Sint-Lenaarts near Brecht.

Grandfather Jozef, born in 1894, had been conscripted in 1914 immediately before the outbreak of the Great War. Two of the three sons (of a family of eleven) had been able to escape this fate: the eldest son had escaped by good fortune when drawing lots, the second one had been 'bought out'. But after 1909 every family had to supply at least one soldier, and from 1913 on, when his turn came, every young man had to do his military service.

Thank God, more has remained of him than just the photo of a serious young man with big ears, wearing an oversized coat and army boots. My grandfather, who had attended secondary school in Hoogstraten, had learnt enough French to understand the orders of the French-speaking officers, and so he survived – unlike many of his Flemish fellow soldiers. It was no wonder that he became a *'flamingant'* in the trenches of the front line, although we do not know if he was ever active in the Flemish Movement. He served at the IJzer front for three years. In 1917 he was taken prisoner of war, after a German soldier's advice to throw away his rifle saved him from an untimely death. He was one of the last men to return to his village in 1919, having been held as a prisoner of war in Germany for two years. He had worked there with farmers who treated him well, and kept him in ignorance of the cease-fire in order to keep him on longer. Or was it the farmer's daughter who caused Grandpa Jozef's hesitation in going home? At any event, November 11 became *the* feast day of the year for my grandfather; on that day a neighbour even had to come and milk the cows as Grandpa would not work.

His loyalty to Flanders did not prevent him from marrying a young woman with a 'Walloon' heart. But in contrast to my great-aunt's two children, his offspring were not brought up in French. Naturally, Grandpa Jozef attended the annual IJzer pilgrimage (*IJzerbedevaart*) on the last weekend of August: a gathering ostensibly to commemorate the unnumbered casualties among Flemish soldiers in the Great War, but in reality also an assembly which was used, and abused, for Flemish nationalistic purposes.

Things could never return to what they had been before those terrible years, neither for my Walloon nor my Flemish grandparents: on August 4, 1914 the German army had invaded Belgium near Gemmenich, moved forward via the Voer area, and built a pontoon bridge at Visé. Great-great-grandfather François Larue (1842-1914), aged 72, and his daughters crept on hands and knees through the cornfields to the nearby Netherlands. François Larue never made it; we don't know where he is buried. Towards the end of the war, my grandmother Julia, 15 years old, became ill, stopped school and was sent to recover with her aunts in Warsage and Sint-Pieters-Voeren.

The Second World War was endured patiently and without injury by my mother's family, farmers who had enough to eat, until one lunchtime in March 1945 when a V1 which had been shaken off course by heavy firing in Brecht, fell on the neighbours' house. My grandparents' home was partly destroyed, but, by a miracle, my mother's family were spared.

My grandmother Julia was a woman who followed the royal household closely and had a soft spot for Astrid, the queen who had died young in a car accident in 1935. It was in her Sunday missal that I found a prayer inscribed: "Leopoldum and a Prayer for our King". My mother also remembers the so-called Royal Question, and how the Flemish population was influenced by Catholic schools and parish priests, until a vast majority voted for the King's return. For her the cause of the troubles around Leopold III was his marriage with Lilian Baels, in the first year of the Second World War. For my grandfather Jozef the fact that King Albert spoke French to his soldiers at the front during the First World War was sufficient to condemn the monarchy.

My grandfather, as a member of the 'Farmers' Union' (*Boerenbond*), and my mother as a member of the 'Farmers' Girls' (*Boerinnenjeugd*), took part in the mass demonstrations of the so-called School War in 1955, calling for the "salvation of the soul of the child". They travelled from the Noorderkempen to Brussels in order to join the protesting crowds. My mother still remembers the slogan "Down with Collard!", who was the Socialist minister for education at that time, and who wanted drastically (and for good reasons) to increase the state's control over Catholic education. It must have been pretty chaotic on that day in Brussels, a day when even my respectable grandfather was seen to be pulling up paving stones to use as weapons.

After the death of great-aunt Martha a couple of years ago, the nephews and nieces from Flanders and Wallonia met for the last time. The funeral took place in Sint-Genesius-Rode, an officially Dutch-speaking community (but with special protection rights for the substantial minority of French speakers) south of Brussels, where her daughter happened to live. None of her nephews and nieces was really bilingual. Even the grandchildren of the three Larue sisters, when they tried to make themselves understood to each other, found themselves falling back on their best school French on the one hand, or the little Dutch they had learnt at their Walloon schools on the other. Thus the family had grown apart, and with the death of aunt Martha it was dispersed for good.

Hand in hand with Belgium's development into a modern nation with a sophisticatedly multiple identity, this one very characteristic Belgian family has, little by little, been dispersing.

A Nation: Belgian, Walloon and/or Flemish Identity?

What does my little family chronicle tell us about the issue of Belgian identity? My great-grandfather, Victor Larue from Warsage, who had been sent to Flanders thanks to his Walloon origins, his French mother tongue, and his knowledge of Dutch, and who proceeded to build his career in Flanders, was perhaps the most Belgian of all my ancestors. His daughters were perfectly bilingual, though they only benefited from that in their later working lives. Yet in spite of having been born and having spent all their lives in Flanders, the three of them remained 'Walloon girls' at heart. It was not their place of birth, but rather their emotional experiences that determined their identity, in addition perhaps to the fact that they were the children of an immigrant.

My grandfather Jozef was quite different: he developed a Flemish identity during the war years (1914-1918), which he then passed on to my mother and perhaps, through her, also to me. But still, every member of my mother's family was Belgian, on another, perhaps higher level, just as we all are or will become Europeans one level further. However, regional identity (which doesn't mean simply one's place of birth) plays an important part, after all: Warsage is very close to the Voer district, which is a bilingual, or rather trilingual area. These villages too have, in part, contributed to the identity of the members of my family.

The process of Belgian constitutional reform started in 1970 and was formally completed in the fifth state reform of 2001, but this does not signify the end of the process. The 'new' Belgium, or rather its Walloon, Flemish and German-speaking regions, are on their way to merge with greater Europe. Which means that while strongly adhering to their newly developed identity as Walloons, as Flemings, or as German-speaking East Belgians, in a future 'Europe of regions', these regions will no longer experience their 'Belgian' identity as the apex or keystone of the complex structure of their various identities.

A History
From the Kingdom of the Netherlands
to Federal Belgium

How did it all come about? The following selection of dates and facts may help to understand the family stories told above and provide some historical background.

1815-1830
Kingdom of the Netherlands and Preparation for the Revolution

At the Congress of Vienna (1815), the great powers (France, England, Prussia, Austria-Hungary, Russia) decided that Belgium should be part of the Kingdom of the Netherlands, ruled by King William I, monarch of the latter from 1813 on. The ancient ecclesiastical princedom of Liège with its counties Stavelot and Boulogne, which belonged to the Holy Roman Empire as an independent state from 985 until 1794, and had then been annexed by the French, now also became a part of the Kingdom of the Netherlands.

The Belgian bourgeoisie and nobility in the South, did not feel integrated into the authoritarian regime of King William I. Even though the South had twice the population of the North, only just half of all parliamentary positions were filled by Southerners. The freedom of the press was limited; education was under state control, a counter measure to the Catholic tradition in the South. For the Church there had a firm grip on children's education, founding a system that extended right through from primary schools to the Catholic University of Leuven, founded in 1425. William's language policy was to encourage the use of Dutch in regions and domains where French had previously been dominant. The French language, highly regarded by the Belgian elite and middle classes, had been the language which every educated child had the opportunity and the obligation to learn. It was the language of the well-off social classes and of anyone who wished to 'belong'. For these reasons it was difficult for the people to accept this strange Dutch language, spoken by the protestants of the North. The Belgian elite demanded the freedom to use their language of preference: French.

The blossoming of the Dutch language in certain fields during these fifteen years of the Kingdom of the Netherlands was the main reason for the Flemish Movement being established in the way it was. This movement started shortly after 1830 as a literary, philological and cultural one, supported by, among others, those who had been educated during this Dutch period and had thus familiarised themselves with the more northern language. If this period had not taken place, the Flemish might have succeeded in developing their own standard language. This language, while it would of course have remained closely related to the Dutch spoken in Holland, might nevertheless have had a distinctive form. It is, however, more probable that the official language, French, would have completely suppressed the Flemish dialects of the region, presumably in the same drastic manner as the Flemish dialects were suppressed in the part of Flanders belonging to France.

The fact remains, that the language of the North, which underwent a huge amount of influence from Brabant immigrants in the sixteenth and seventeenth centuries, possessed enough defining characteristics to be classified as Standard Dutch. The pronunciation stayed closer to the written language in Flanders than in the Netherlands. There was certainly little enthusiasm for simply adopting the Dutch from the North, but on the other hand the pressure to be associated with an already existing 'standard' language was powerful. United we stood firmly against the threat of French. However, the North never felt compelled to involve itself in the language struggles in Belgium after independence.

In 1828, Catholics and Liberals formed a union under a joint programme. It was called a 'monster coalition', an alliance which gave Belgium its coat of arms and its motto: *"L'union fait la force, eendracht maakt macht"* (Unity gives strength).

The Catholic Church successfully shook off the interference of William I in its day-to-day affairs, and the Belgian population remained heavily controlled by the church from the pulpit and in the confessional until well into the 1960s. The Liberals had little option but to cooperate with this powerful Catholicism, although, at the same time, William I's promotion of the industrialisation of Belgium gained him the support of those Belgian Liberals who were the direct beneficiaries of this process. The working classes, on the other hand, were not content with this development at all: industrialisation and famine brought periodic unemployment and growing unrest in Brussels.

1830-1831
The Revolution and the Foundation of the Monarchy

All this led to a 'revolution'. It wasn't a revolution from the start, but it wasn't just a spontaneous putsch by a small dissatisfied group either: it grew from the widespread discontent. The stubborn refusal of William I not to give in to the demands of the bourgeoisie and nobility turned the uprising into a revolution, which led to the separation from the North and finally brought independence to the newly created Belgian state.

From August 3, 1830 Daniel Auber's opera *La Muette de Portici* in the *Théâtre de la Monnaie* in Brussels was forbidden because of its alleged 'bad influence' on the audience, but on the famous evening of August 25 it was again on the programme. The main reason was the tenor Jean-Francois Lafeuillade's famous aria: "*Amour sacré de la patrie, rends-nous l'audace et la fierté; à mon pays je dois la vie, il me devra sa liberté*" (Sacred love of my country, give us courage and pride, my country gave me my life, I will give it freedom). Upon hearing these powerful words, the young audience felt compelled to act and thus took to the streets of Brussels to revolt. This revolt spread to the working classes and would last until the evening of August 26.

Step by step, the uprising in the streets of Brussels developed into a full-blown revolution, followed in the next days by 'famine uprisings' in Louvain, Liège, Verviers, and elsewhere. On September 23 volunteers from all over the country joined the rebellion in Brussels, and on September 27 William ordered his soldiers to avoid further bloodshed. Consequently, the Dutch army withdrew.

A 'Provisional Government' formed by the city of Brussels administration in order to keep the peace, rapidly declared independence on October 4, 1830. This government consisted of Liberals and Catholics who now worked together to dampen down the revolt of the working classes in the city. On November 3, 1830 the first elections took place for a National Congress, on the basis of tax suffrage. In total (only) 30,000 Belgian men voted. This was followed by the first full meeting of the Congress on November 10, 1830, a gathering of 200 members from the bourgeoisie and nobility.

On November 4, 1830 the great powers of the time convened a conference in London to draft a peace agreement between the Netherlands and Belgium, but they would not fully succeed in this until 1839.

On February 7, 1831 the National Congress accepted the Belgian constitution, which was a very modern constitution for its time. Legislative power lay in the hands of the Chamber of Representatives and the more elitist Senate, which passed the laws and the State's budgets. The King still had to ratify the laws to bring them into force. The Senate later evolved into a more democratic chamber the role of which, like that of many upper houses, is to review and reflect on issues and bills. Executive power lay in the hands of the government: the King and his ministers. Every law had to be signed by the Government, and also by the King, the latter surviving, as in many countries, as a mere formality nowadays.

On July 21, 1831 King Leopold I (1831-1865) arrived in Calais from London, touching Belgian soil for the first time in De Panne, and happily announcing his arrival throughout the land. In Brussels, he swore the oath to the constitution. To the great powers, Leopold, son of Duke Franz of Saxe-

Coburg-Gotha, appeared to be the ideal king for a buffer state such as Belgium. This was thanks to a curriculum vitae which suited the powers down to the ground: born into the German aristocracy, the widower of the British princess Charlotte and an ex-officer of the Russian imperial army who had fought for the Tsar against Napoleon. The throne was offered to him in June, and although he found Belgium rather a small country, he decided that he who cannot honour small things is not worth greater ones. And this decision turned out to be the right one: he became the father of a monarchy which has outlived most other European ones and which offered him many attractive possibilities. For largely diplomatic and dynastic reasons, he married in 1832 princess Louise-Marie de Orléans, daughter of the King of France.

Shortly after King Leopold I's ascent to the throne, the King of the Netherlands made his final attempt on August 2, 1831 to win back Belgium by rejecting the proposals laid down by the Conference of London. This campaign initially went well for the Netherlands, but when France came to Belgium's rescue, the Dutch had to abandon their efforts on August 12.

On September 8, 1831 the first parliament was elected.

1831-1855
The Young State in Search of National Identity

In 1839 a peace agreement with the Netherlands was reached: the 24 Articles of the London Conference were accepted by both countries out of sheer necessity. The Netherlands agreed to Belgium's independence, but the great powers forced Belgium to remain neutral, in order to prevent this small country from collaboration with either one of her neighbours. King Leopold I had also to abandon his dream of creating a somewhat larger Belgium and thus to be content with a kingdom the borders of which had been drawn by the great powers. The province of Limburg was divided into Dutch and Belgian Limburg: after belonging to Belgium for nine years the eastern Limburgers became Dutch again. More importantly, Belgium did not gain the Schelde estuary.

Unitary Belgium received a first serious blow in 1847. In those first 17 years the young state had been trying in vain to create a feeling of unity between Catholics and Liberals, between the rising bourgeoisie and the traditional nobility, and between provinces and cities with a strong tradition of local autonomy, some of which had never been part of the same territory before 1795. A way to assert this national unity was to put the Flemish golden age of the Middle Ages centre stage in the historiography of the new Belgian State. But did this ever exist?

The 'monster coalition' held out as long as the mutual enemy, the Netherlands, remained potentially predatory. As soon as relations with the northern neighbour had normalised, however, things internal began to fall apart. The period of unionism came to an end in 1847, and an exclusively Liberal government ensued.

Belgium remained unscathed by the February revolution in Paris (1848) in part by assuming a distant attitude to the events. This was a sign of aversion to France, a country which Belgium regarded as a dangerous neighbour, with annexation always felt as a distinct threat. However, thanks to the decision of the Liberal government to extend electoral suffrage, the lower middle classes remained immune to any calls for revolution coming from turbulent France.

This was also the time of romanticism in which nationalism had a special part. Sources such as Philip Blommaert's *Notes on the Neglect of the Netherlandic Language (Aanmerkingen over de verwaerloozing der Nederduitsche tael)* of 1832 could support the opinion that it is not an anachronism to say that the process of federalisation began together with the creation of Belgium. But in those days the Flemish population didn't take much notice of the 'Flemish Movement'. They were suffering from a famine caused by poor grain and potato harvests which plagued Flanders the same way as they did Ireland. An important part of the population emigrated to Wallonia, France, the United States, or Canada to escape their hopeless prospects. In 1847/48 typhoid and cholera raged.

The Congress of Dutch Language and Literature, organised in 1849 in Ghent, was the first meeting of the North and the South since 1830. Up to 1912, 32 more such congresses would take place. However, the original aim of giving the Dutch language more prestige and power within Belgium by cooperating closely with the Northern neighbours, failed. The Dutch regarded the Flemish issue as Belgium's own political problem. This attitude changed only gradually after the establishment of the 'Language Union' (*Taalunie*) in 1980.

1855-1880
The End of '*l'utopie de l'unité de langage*'

When in 1855 the 25th anniversary of Belgium was celebrated, the Liberal period had come to an end. Now the Catholics took over. In 1880, '*l'utopie de l'unité de langage*' was given up for good. Legislation on official language use began to appear from 1873 onwards. These language laws acknowledged Dutch, French, and – much later, in 1962 – German as official languages. Since independence, Article 23 of the constitution had recognised the freedom of language, which in practice meant that anyone could speak what he or she wanted anywhere, while consecrating at the same time the exclusive place of French in public life. Whatever happened, at certain moments in life, an educated person would always speak French, even at home. It was only with the establishment of laws on language use that this situation could be brought to an end. So, gradually language legislation was introduced, culminating in 1963 in the legal acknowledgement of borders between the languages within Belgium itself. This development took time: Dutch was recognised as official language for administrative matters in 1878, and Dutch-speaking secondary schools were set up in the Flemish provinces in 1883, but in reality most tuition still went on in French, with only some subjects taught in Dutch, until well into the twentieth century.

After a reign lasting 34 years, King Leopold I died in 1865. His son Leopold II succeeded him for a reign that would last even longer, until 1909. This longevity of Belgian monarchs could be one factor explaining the stability of the state.

1880-1905
In Search of a Greater Kingdom:
The Congo Free State and Democratic Trends in Belgium

In 1885 Congo became the private property of King Leopold II. After a long debate in 1908, more or less pressed by the criticism about the disgraceful state of affairs, the Belgian parliament agreed to take over the country from the King, and Congo officially became a Belgian colony.

In 1885 trade unionists and lawyers founded the Belgian Workers' Party, which later became the Socialist Party. In 1893 the plural vote was introduced, granting one to three votes to each man over 21 years. It turned out to be the first major step towards the democratisation of a state previously largely run by, and for, an upper-class elite. The introduction of the 'De Vriendt/Coremans law of equality' meant that Dutch was recognised as an official language of Belgium, along with French. Dutch officially received the same status as French in the Constitution.

1905-1930
Before and after World War I

In 1909 King Leopold II was succeeded by Albert I.
Compulsory education was finally passed in 1914. Children would in theory be required by law to attend primary school until the age of 14, the schools being run by the Catholic church or by the local authorities. It would in fact take a long time before this social breakthrough became a reality for every family. It is still possible in today's Belgium to be considered in 'compulsory education' without attending school.

Despite Belgium's neutrality, Germany invaded the country in 1914. Belgium had no other choice than to fight for its existence under threat of annexation by, or submission to Germany. As Sophie de Schaepdrijver's contribution to this volume explains, 'Harmless, Trusting Little Belgium' played an important role in the First World War, especially as a symbolic victim. Belgium was portrayed by the Allied propaganda as a courageous and heroic country led by the exceptional King Albert I, 'the Knight King'. The American food relief operation set up by Herbert Hoover spared the population the horrors of starvation and famine. In 1920, following the

Versailles Treaty, the German-speaking region of Eupen-Malmedy-Sankt Vith region became part of Belgium.

At the parliamentary elections in 1919, a universal single-vote system was introduced for all men over 21 years of age. In 1921 the Constitution granted women the right to vote in local elections, and war widows were also allowed to vote in parliamentary elections. Only in 1948 did all women obtain the right (and the duty) to vote in provincial and national elections.

1930-1955
Before and after World War II

In 1932, a general 'Dutchification' of education and administration in the Flemish provinces took place. This, together with the introduction of compulsory schooling up to sixteen years of age in 1935 (later extended to eighteen), was an important step in the build-up of the self-confidence of Flanders. The one-language status of Flanders and Wallonia was established, and the three language areas – Dutch, French, German – were recognised, the boundaries of which could still easily be changed, however, according to the outcomes of each national census. Since 1963 the language borders can only be changed by law.

In the immediate post-war period after 1945, Belgium was not only preoccupied with recovering from the war. The so-called Royal Question deeply divided the country between the largely Catholic supporters of King Leopold III, and their opponents, the Socialists, Liberals and Communists. Thanks to their clever use of the image of King Leopold III, the Christian People's Party gained its first outright majority since 1914. Divisions and hatred between Leopoldists and Anti-Leopoldists ran so deep that Belgium barely escaped a civil war. Only when the Christian People's Party convinced the King to renounce his constitutional role was the country's unity preserved. In 1951 King Leopold III officially stepped down, in favour of his son, the 20 year-old Crown Prince Baudouin.

After the sufferings of World War II, and the Royal Question, another political problem divided the country: the so-called School War. The Catholic parliamentary opposition and its 'pillar' in the civil society bitterly contested the Socialist and Liberal government's proposal that the state take full control over secondary schools. In 1955 the Catholic politicians managed to mobilise 250,000 people for demonstrations in Brussels against the government. This crisis was only resolved in the so-called School Pact of November 6, 1958, based on the principle of free choice of schools by parents. In effect this educational crisis led to an improvement of both Catholic and state school systems.

1955-1980
Towards a Europe of Regions

January 1, 1958 European economic integration started with the creation of the ECCS out of 6 countries: France, Germany, Italy, Luxemburg, the Netherlands and Belgium.

In 1960 the Belgian colony of the Congo obtained its independence. Unprepared for this step, it soon tumbled into chaos.

An important step to federalism was to delineate the linguistic borders between Dutch-, French-, German-speaking and bilingual Dutch-French territories in 1962/63, formally confirming the existence of four linguistic regions defined for administrative purposes. The Dutch-French linguistic boundary can be changed only with a special majority in both language groups of the National Parliament. Economically Flanders entered a period of economic boom, attracting large foreign investment because of its human resources, geographical situation and ports, which made it from 1965 onward the most important industrial region in Belgium. In contrast, Wallonia with its outdated heavy industry went into decline.

The State Reform Bill in 1970 was the first in a series of steps towards federalism. The Dutch-, French-, and German-speaking Communities gained autonomy in cultural matters, and the foundation of the three Regions, Wallonia, Flanders and Brussels, which were based on the territory principle, eased the path towards economic self-government.

1980-2005
25 Years of Federalism: Belgium on its Way to Separation?

In the Second State Reform of 1980 the names of the communities were changed to reflect the extension of responsibilities. They are now officially called the Flemish Community, the French Community and the German-speaking Community, each with a council (parliament) and an executive (government). At the same time, two regions, the Flemish and the Walloon Region, each equally with a council and a government, were created. Then the council and the government of the Flanders Region and of the Flemish Community were merged; in Flanders there is only one government and one council for both the Community and the Region.

The Third State Reform took place in 1988/89: The Brussels-Capital Region was created, also with its own council/parliament and executive.

The Communities received more devolved power especially in the field of education. The Regions were further consolidated.

July 14, 1993 the phrase "Belgium is a federal state" was formally inserted into the constitution. The first clause of the first Article now reads: "Belgium is a federal state which consists of Communities and Regions". King Baudouin died a few days after he signed this Fourth Reform of the constitution. Two weeks later, August 3, 1993, he was succeeded by his brother, the Prince of Liège, now King Albert II.

The Fifth State Reform was completed in 2001: The Communities and the Regions gained the powers and responsibilities which they hold today.

On July 21, 2005 Belgium celebrated with its National Holiday the 175 years since its foundation, and 25 years of federalism. In this situation, when some see a visible threat of complete disintegration of the country, others stress the unity of the country time and again. But a return to unitary Belgium is neither possible nor desirable.

By way of conclusion

Twenty-five years after the Second Constitutional Reform we celebrate federal Belgium because it is this structure, preceded by a quest that lasted 175 years and that is still unfinished today, that led to the establishment of an orderly state in which there is (more) room for a diversity of linguistic and cultural communities. Yet the journey is not over. We can hope that the past will show us the way somewhat more quickly this time. But apparently this has not been possible for Belgium:

it seems that only chaos and obscurity have been feasible for a state like ours. We came through, though, to wander into Europe.

How truly pluralist this state will become, is hard to say for in Belgium too, multiculturalism poses many problems which have not yet been solved. There thus remain many challenges whilst at least some tentative maps towards progress have been drawn. Part of being Belgian today is to feel a certain modest pride over our extensive experience when it comes to engaging with compromise in order to reach an ever-changing consensus.

SOPHIE DE SCHAEPDRIJVER

Champion or Stillbirth?
The symbolic uses of Belgium in the
Great War

Introduction

Hard as it is to imagine in a deconstructionist age, and in a culture profoundly sceptical over all forms of tricolour enthusiasm, Belgium has lived a brief career as a symbol in wartime – to be more precise during World War One, when the country was exalted by one camp and rejected by the other in terms that said much about the way societies mentally geared up for that terrible war – and not a lot about Belgium itself. This contribution, then, addresses not so much the issue of *Belgium Revealed*[1] as it does the question of Belgium buried under layers of rhetoric, ever since August 4, 1914, when the country was invaded by the German Empire.

The Western front, breeding-ground for irony and tragedy, was, as is well known, a series of struggles over the – often barely perceptible – high ground, from Hill 60 to Vimy Ridge. In a parallel fashion, the 'war of meaning' shaped itself as a struggle over the *moral* high ground. (This war of meaning, just like the actual front, did not see much movement over the next four years, but it did mobilise a great deal of energies.) And it so happened that Belgium was a first locus of that struggle. Indeed it was the exemplary locus of that struggle: it was over Belgium that positions were staked out from the first.

The reason, then, for taking a closer look at the vast outpouring of international rhetoric over Belgium, is that this rhetoric provides us with a privileged area of inquiry, addressing as it does questions crucial to an era of citizen armies (what is the war being fought *for* and what is it being fought *against*?). It is no exaggeration to say that, on both sides, Belgium temporarily became shorthand for the moral issues of the war. A tall order for what had been, until then, a hazily defined national entity.

The Russian novelist Konstantin Paustovskii recounts in his memoirs how, during the summer of 1914, when "all of Moscow sang songs praising the defence of Liège", he read Belgian literature to seek to "explain the bravery of this people. But I found no explanation in the convoluted poems of Verhaeren, or the lifeless novels of Rodenbach, or the plays by Maeterlinck that sounded as if he had written them in his sleep."[2] A modern and heterogeneous society, Belgium was not easily imagined internationally. It had a much less distinct international image than other small European countries – the Netherlands, Portugal, Denmark, Serbia.

Perhaps this elusive quality contributed toward making it so malleable a symbol once war broke out, a vessel into which any kind of war rhetoric could be poured. For the one side, it became a symbol of all that was to be exalted in Europe; and for the other side, it stood for all that was to be rejected in Europe. Both attitudes toward Belgium-as-symbol – exaltation on the one hand, rejection on the other – translate the respective imaginings of the war in the respective societies; they expressed underlying assumptions as to the deepest issues of the struggle, that is to say, what values were considered threatened and where the threat was held to emanate from. In this sense, the discourse on Belgium was to provide the template for the discourse on subsequent acts of war.

In what follows, I will concentrate on the 'Belgian discourse' of two belligerent cultures, the British and the German. In both cases, the Belgian element loomed large. (It was prominent enough in French war rhetoric, at least in 1914-1915, although, for obvious reasons, in invaded France the dimension of national defence was sufficiently self-evident that no third countries had to be evoked to strengthen the mobilisation message.) To say that the 'Belgian discourse' of Britain and that of Germany articulated diametrically opposed ideologies would be an exaggeration, but they certainly indicated divergent visions of Europe, as I hope to show. [3]

The 'Belgian discourse' of Britain and Germany

There is something striking about the following list of items: the invasion of Belgium, the sinking of the Lusitania, the use of poison gas, the execution of Nurse Edith Cavell, unrestricted submarine warfare. All of these highly publicised acts of war – one might call them 'tropes of indignation' – were committed (or, in the case of gas, committed *first*) by Germany. Throughout the 'war of meaning', what one might call the initiative of indignation invariably came from Britain. The German discourse was consistently unable to get hold of the initiative; it was unable, for instance, to elevate the economic blockade of Germany, with its string of misery inflicted on civilians, into a comparable paradigm of fiendishness. As a result, the German discourse was perpetually forced into the defensive, which further reinforced a theme already forcefully present, to wit, that of Germany's right to self-defence as overriding all possible objections.

The choreography of this 'dance of rhetorics' between Germany and Britain was first, and lastingly, articulated in the case of Belgium's invasion. An act to which British official opinion, and indeed British public opinion, reacted with great vehemence. The academic Mary Stocks, a member (if the term applies) of the Bloomsbury group, was later to recall the general "revulsion of feeling on learning of the Belgian invasion, which brought [us all] into wholehearted support of the war effort [and] (...) was seen as a monstrous, wicked, unprovoked act of aggression against a small neutral country which we were honour bound to assist." [4] In other words, the case of Belgium, an innocent being bullied, mobilised Victorian/Edwardian notions of honour and dictated a line of duty. The war which had so very recently been considered a mere "general scrap" [5] now made eminent sense. *Punch* magazine published a famous cartoon entitled "Bravo, Belgium!", depicting Belgium as a brave country lad defending his territory against Germany – a stick-wielding bully, trouser pocket a-dangle with a string of sausages.

London music-hall singers got standing ovations with a rousing anthem called *Bravo! Little Belgium*:

Bravo! Little Belgium, it's proud we are of you
Bravo! Little Belgium, you'd the pluck to see it through
Hats off to little Belgium,
You're a fighting race sublime!
Your flag is still unfurled
In front of all the world
And we're with you – all the time! [6]

Bravo, Belgium! [7]

The war was no longer an undifferentiated scrap. It had a clear aggressor and aggressee and could be reinterpreted as a crusade.

This indignation, and its wider importance for the world's overall judgements on the war, were not lost on German opinion. As the pedagogue Friedrich Wilhelm Foerster would later state, "it was on the basis of [the invasion of Belgium] that the world came to judge the question of war guilt in its entirety."[8] As a consequence the need for self-justification was keenly felt; and this self-justification couched itself in terms of the overwhelming importance of self-defence. Chancellor von Bethmann Hollweg in his Reichstag speech of August 4 – held within hours of the invasion – admitted the iniquity of the invasion of a neutral country, but invoked the urgency of self-defence for a nation fighting for its life. Later that day, Bethmann vented his exasperation over Britain's entry into the war to the British Ambassador by fulminating against the "Scrap of Paper"(*Fetzen Papier*) that was the Belgian Treaty of Neutrality of 1839, which pledged both Germany and Britain to respect and defend Belgium's territorial integrity (and over the breaking of which Britain now declared war).

These statements, like that of Mary Stocks, are replete with deeper assumptions: Bethmann did acknowledge that the invasion of Belgium was a breach of the rules, but a breach of the rules rendered necessary by the emergency of the situation. The group-person Germany – the 'we' of Bethmann's speech – was held to be in danger; in existential danger to boot (*"Feinde ringsum"* – surrounded by enemies – as one poem put it).[9] Indeed, Bethmann transvalued the situation into presenting 'us' as the real aggressee – which danger gave 'us' the right to self-defence by all means available, disregarding earlier covenants as so many 'scraps of paper' rendered insignificant by the colossal importance of the moment.

Bethmann Hollweg's statement was consistent with much of German public opinion. (Wilhelm Muehlon, the renegade Krupp director, on August 6 noted his shock over seeing the invasion of Belgium justified, even approved, by all around him. [10]) Diplomatically, it was an epic blunder. The 'Scrap of Paper' phrase was immediately made to serve the emergent rhetoric of British war aims. (One war poster, titled "The Scrap of Paper" prominently displayed the 1839 Treaty with the words: "The Germans have broken their pledged Word and devastated Belgium. Help to keep your Country's Honour bright by restoring Belgium her Liberty." [11]) Britain could now be imagined as defending the rule of law, the cause of Right against Might. A stance that is very well expressed in a position paper with the title *Why We Are At War*, issued in October 1914 by a group of Oxford historians. It contained the declaration that

> *[W]e must fight Prussia (...) in the noblest cause for which men can fight. That cause is the public law of Europe, as a sure shield and buckler of all nations, great and small, and especially the small. To the doctrine of the almightiness of the state – to the doctrine that all means are justified which are, or seem, necessary to its self-preservation, we oppose the doctrine of a European society, or at least a European comity of nations, within which all states stand; we oppose the doctrine of a public law of Europe, by which all states are bound to respect the covenants they have made. We will not and cannot tolerate the view that nations are 'in the state and posture of gladiators' in their relations one with another; we stand for the reign of law.*

The British mission, then, was defined as championing civic virtue, showing the world how to 'play the game' by the rules, which was the only manner in which civilisation could be conceived. Britain was imagined to be the eternal upholder of these values: 'We are a people in whose blood the cause of law is the vital element. It is no new thing in our history that we should fight for that cause.'[12]

The first German reaction to international opprobrium consisted of a systematic campaign of casting doubt on Belgium's very neutrality. Belgium – or so it was claimed – had before the war concluded secret treaties with France and Britain, thus forfeiting any claim to innocence; on a more structural level, the Belgian State had been created as an outpost of French and British interests and so had from its inception been an anti-German presence; Germany in invading it had therefore been attacking not a neutral but an enemy, a stealthy enemy at that. Once again, treaties and established rules were unveiled as so much cant, devised by an envious and devious world to keep Germany down.

So for a while, the question of Belgium's neutrality was made to carry the full weight of the European rule of law. In British rhetoric, Belgium's neutrality signified international justice, which in turn stood for Civilisation as a whole. In German rhetoric, the contention that Belgium's neutrality was a lie strengthened the notion that what passed for international justice was in reality an anti-German hoax, as indeed were so many of the values of Anglo-French civilisation. 'Civilisation' itself (*Zivilisation*) was portrayed as essentially foreign as compared to the German quality of culture (*Kultur*). *Zivilisation* was external, formal, not to say hypocritical; *Kultur* represented an altogether deeper, more interior quality, concerned as it was with "inner freedom, with authenticity, with truth rather than sham, with essence as opposed to appearance".[13] The impassioned distinction made in Germany between *Zivilisation* and *Kultur* predates the conflict, but it was given fresh life and urgency by the war.[14]

The emphasis, in British public discourse, on the rule of law as the central issue of the war led to the exaltation of Belgium – considered the figurehead in the struggle to uphold this rule of law. The Belgian government, in the night of August 2, 1914, had rejected the German ultimatum demanding unimpeded passage into France for the German armies. It had refused because its neutral status did not permit such a concession. This refusal had brought it into open war with Germany, resulting in an unequal and devastating struggle. Which had the one advantage of elevating Belgium to exalted levels in the British imagination. (At least since Tennyson's Charge of the Light Brigade (1855), British patriotic culture had linked heroism in battle to the unequal – and therefore by definition chivalrous – nature of that battle.[15]) Belgium's plight at the hands of the German invader (see below) lent a further aura of heroism to its defence of its neutrality. Paeans to 'Brave Little Belgium' waxed accordingly dithyrambic. Great praise was lavished on a country which the British public before the war had mainly known for its prostitution scandals and its misdeeds in the Congo, if at all. Those days were past, as evidenced in statements such as the one made in December 1914 by Joseph Herman Hertz, Head of the United Hebrew Congregations of the British Empire:

> *Only that nation can be called cultured ... which by its living, and, if need be, by its dying, vindicates the eternal values of life – conscience, honour, liberty. Judged by this test, two of the littlest of peoples, Judaea in ancient times and Belgium to-day, and not their mighty and ruthless oppressors, are among the chief defenders of culture, champions of the sacred heritage of man.*[16]

The Belgian Knight, Fighting a Bird of Prey [17]

Little Belgium had become a principle, an idea, destined even to outlive the demise of the actual Belgian state if it came to that; a principle embodying an entire array of 'eternal' (Victorian/Edwardian) values – honour, liberty, all that constituted the "sacred heritage of man". And also the defence of true culture: note how Rabbi Hertz' references to "culture" are a sneer – one among many in Entente discourse – at the now notorious German conception of *Kultur*.

The British exaltation of Belgium fitted a context of Right-against-Might rhetoric. In an analogous manner did the German emphasis on the unveiling of enemy hypocrisy require the rejection of Belgium as a reality. (Which incidentally explains why, in German visual propaganda, there are no allegoric representations of Belgium, not even negative ones.) As the economist Werner Sombart famously wrote in the (left-liberal) *Berliner Tageblatt*, "Belgium is a still-born product of European diplomacy."[18] At the heart of this statement lies the charge of artificiality. Belgium was not a nation, nor a people, nor a country with a *raison-d'être*; it was a mere artefact, and could not be otherwise, for in the last analysis, everything wrought by shallow civilisation was but an artefact. Belgium's existence had from the start been nothing but a legal fiction, destined to shrivel in the face of the fiercer truths of war – a legal fiction in the service of Anglo-French interests, a link in the chain that encircled and suffocated Germany.

Meanwhile, the invasion of Belgium – in German war discourse, a heroic measure to break the suffocating chain – had caused the death of over five thousand Belgian civilians at the hands of German troops. These massacres[19] harshly contradicted widely held beliefs that modern warfare would be a tidy affair, sparing civilians; they caused international shock.

A *Franc-tireur* Attack near Herve [20]

On the German side, the carnage was justified with a counteraccusation: Belgian civilians had fought a guerilla war (*Franktireurkrieg*) against the invading troops. This accusation was false: no such mobilisation of Belgian civilians took place. But that which the historians John Horne and Alan Kramer have called the 'myth complex' of the Belgian snipers' war, or *franc-tireur* war, slotted seamlessly into a by now consecrated image of Germany-at-war: a nation attacked on all sides in stealthy ways. The Belgian *franc-tireur*, that mythical figure, served as an emblem of the forces that threatened Germany, forces that were both ruthless and treacherous but cried foul when honestly fought or sternly punished. (In response to Entente accusations of Germany's crimes against humanity, a disgusted Thomas Mann took to referring to 'the rights of man' between dismissive quotation marks. [21])

In the words of the manifesto *An Die Kulturwelt!* launched in October by 93 German intellectuals,

> *again and again, (...) the Belgians shot at our troops from ambush, mutilated the wounded, and murdered physicians who were occupied in their work of mercy. It is not possible for one to misrepresent the truth more contemptibly, than by suppressing accounts of the crimes of these assassins, in order that the just punishment which they suffered may be made to appear a crime committed by the Germans.* [22]

Elsewhere, the *Manifesto* accused the "enraged population" of Leuven of having "stealthily" slunk up to German troops" billets to attack them. [23] Belgians, in accounts such as these, were presented as pathologically untrustworthy and barbaric; as capable, down to the last man, women and child, of unspeakable atrocities – cutting off the fingers of the wounded to retrieve rings, gauging out their eyes, hammering rusty nails in sleeping soldiers' skulls, nailing severed heads to church doors at the demand of their priests, and so on. Women and children were far from innocent, priests the worst of all. [24] The franc-tireur mythology, as John Horne and Alan Kramer write, grew into "one expression of the larger war trauma of German society." [25] It also presented Belgium as the perfect antithesis to Germany in terms of warfare. It fuelled a kind of strident self-congratulation, positing a flattering difference between two modes of fighting, which can be summarised as follows:

German mode of fighting	Belgian mode of fighting
disciplined	driven by blind rage
open	by stealth
seeking confrontation in the open field	creeping up from behind
within the ranks of an orderly army	under cover of civilian status
stern	atrocious

No sooner was this difference established than representatives of the Wilhelmine *Bildungsbürgertum* rushed in to pour it into a coherent cultural theory. The Belgian mentality, it was argued, was essentially not quite sane, and certainly not quite 'cultured'. (One pan-German commentator compared the Belgians to the Herero people in Germany's South-West African colony. [26]) Two German art historians, trying to fit in reports of Belgian barbarity with their admiration for Belgian art, merged both phenomena in one theory. "We are of the opinion that Art forms the most intense expression of a people's inner life. (...) A careful look [at Belgian art] reveals to us certain characteristics which we can promptly associate with the Belgian rage, insanity and bestiality being manifested today." From Adriaan Brouwer with his ape-like peasants "who awake from their lethargy only to start screeching like a gang of possessed" to Félicien Rops whose images expressed so accurately "the brutal sensuality, the overheated fantasies of this people", Belgian art, though admirable in itself, offered to Germans "a piece of evidence for Belgian crimes". Thus *Geheimregierungsrat* Prof. Dr. B. Händecke in an essay that stated, in addition, that the Belgian people essentially suffered from "the perverse distortion of something which in and of itself is a quality, namely patriotism." The priest-ridden Belgians' patriotism had degenerated into blind hatred for "every German, considered a heretic to be massacred." Another expert in Belgian art shared this opinion: Belgians' patriotism had grown insane, which explained "the undescribably furious, wild, diabolically cruel behaviour of the Belgian masses' against 'our gallant warriors, fighting so bravely and loyally." In contrast to the Belgians, whose "thoughtless patriotism" rendered them incapable of fighting as disciplined soldiers in army ranks, and who were therefore reduced to lashing out indiscriminately, in a feral and brutal manner, every man for himself. [27]

As a result, the executions of Belgian civilians accused of having shot at the German troops were presented matter-of-factly, and with a further note of self-righteousness, as just punishment for crimes against the rule of law. As the Emperor informed US President Woodrow Wilson in a telegram: "My heart bleeds when I hear how my generals have had to punish the bloodthirsty population". [28]

Arrested *Franc-tireurs*, caught red-handed [28]

Illustrations such as these – and postcards of destroyed cities with captions such as "Leuven after the punishment by our troops" – fuelled overseas indignation. The so-called *German Atrocities*, and inexplicable German reactions to them, were made to serve as proof – if any such proof were needed – of the terrible 'otherness' of the Germans, a people described as bred on the cruel teachings of Nietzsche and national historian Treitschke – names which, in the war discourse, became more familiar to the British public than they had ever been to pre-war Germans. The point was hammered home: Germans were beyond the pale of civilisation. The demonisation of Germany proceeded apace. The Oxford historians cited above had insisted that, for all the authoritarian excesses of Wilhelmine culture, the Germans were still "a great people." [30] But by early 1915 these arguments were giving way to far more lurid representations, even visual obscenities such as the ones collected in the volume *The Kaiser's Garland*

(Wilhelm II bayoneting a naked cherub, and so on). The plight of Belgium became gradually submerged under an ever-thicker layer of myth: 'mere' shootings of civilians became sadistic scenes of torture, the hacking-off of toddler's hands, and rape. Germany's very real subversion of civilised standards in its treatment of Belgium "paled into insignificance once tales became current of raped women and mutilated children."[31]

As, in the escalating logic of war culture, the 'enemy' became the 'Other' – barely human, beyond the pale – the 'rape of Belgium' as a metaphor became the rape of *Belgians*.[32] (This, incidentally, expressed certain contempt for public opinion – as if the 'common man' in an age of mass mobilisation was incapable of grasping the import of abstract duties toward international justice.[33]) Sexual depravity was the surest sign of the enemy's wickedness; and the assault on women brought home – in the literal sense – the urgency of defence. (The *Marseillaise* – that first rallying-cry of citizen armies – had, after all, appealed to exactly these feelings.) In the process, the representation of Belgium, always anthropomorphic, became gynomorphic – with implicit, but insistent, references to rape. "Although one of the smallest and least aggressive of the countries of Europe, the daughter among the nations, Belgium [...] [chose to protect] her right to be mistress in her own house."[34]

There were occasional slides from the gynomorphic to the pornographic. Take, for instance, German troops' use of Belgian civilians as human shields. This well-documented form of violence came to be represented in Entente postcards in a lurid and wholly fictitious manner: bestial-looking Uhlans forcing half-clad women forward.

Why Did She Not Yield? We Would Have Paid[35]

This hyperbole may well have sealed the fate of 'Belgium rhetoric' in Britain. As the war wore on and the rising body count dwarfed the number of Belgian civilian dead, the coarsening of themes and the stepping-up of atrocity-mongering took the edge off the Belgian issue. According to Robert Graves' – admittedly jaundiced – war memoir, by late 1915, "we no longer believed the highly-coloured accounts of German atrocities in Belgium; knowing the Belgians now at first hand." [36] At the Somme, soldiers had been issued a little volume of patriotic marching-songs (the proceeds of which benefited the *Belgian Relief Fund*); one of these songs was to be sung to the lugubrious tune of 'John Brown's Body' and began with the words "Belgium has been harried with fire and with sword ..." Instead the soldiers sang "John Brown's baby's got a pimple on his bum, [...] And the little bugger can't sit down." [37]

The Belgian rhetoric, within the British culture of war, had exhausted itself. To be sure, the restoration of Belgium's independence remained a non-negotiable condition of peace to the end. But the country no longer served as the figurehead of the clash of Right and Might. This was due in part to a mounting impatience with the rolling phrases of 'Liberty' against 'Prussian Militarism'. To be sure, notions of 'duty' endured, but the focus of 'duty' had narrowed. As to the disappearance of Belgium as a theme, the fact that the Belgian refugees were no longer pressed to the nation's bosom the way they had been in 1914 (especially after the introduction of British conscription from January 1916) played a role, as did the realisation that the incessant decrying of Germany's rape of Belgium ultimately "[advertised] the fact that a country Britain had [ostensibly] gone to war to defend had been thoroughly overrun and that attempts to dislodge the invader were proving unavailing." [38] To sum up: the stalemated war was not kind to the notion of Belgium as a 'Champion of Humanity'.

Meanwhile, on the German side, that very continuity of presence on Belgian soil generated an elaborate body of justifications which once more strengthened the notion of Belgium's essential irrelevance. I am referring here to the so-called Flemish Policy (*Flamenpolitik*) which had been devised shortly after the invasion as a means of securing a measure of loyalty at least among one specific group in the occupied country, the Flemings, and as a means of sapping the legitimacy of the Belgian state. [39] (As the Governor-General said in late 1914, "We may have to relinquish Belgium, but we will destroy it through the Flemings." [40]) The Flemish policy was, as far as the occupied country was concerned, a mitigated failure. But the Flemish rhetoric had considerable symbolic value in Germany itself. It presented Belgium as an impossible amalgam of hugely different 'races', a prison of nations in which the humiliated Flemings were subjected to relentless Frenchification. An outrage which the German administration was presently redressing, thus restoring the Flemings to nationhood. This Flemish rhetoric merged with and reinforced the main body of German war rhetoric. It strengthened the notion of Germany's own crusade, a crusade for authenticity, against artificiality. What the British decried as the invasion of a country became an act of liberation of a nation from the clutches of an empire. (Chancellor Bethmann Hollweg told a cheering Reichstag in 1916 that Germany "pledges never again to relinquish our Flemish brethren to Frenchification (*Verwelschung*)".[41]) The Flemings were a related, Germanic nation; their plight in Frenchifying Belgium could be constructed as the plight of all Germanics on the European stage, writ small – that is to say, encirclement, stealthy suffocation, existential danger. In Flanders, the Germans did not find themselves usurping invaded territory; they were on profoundly Germanic soil. Overlooking several centuries of Flemish history, the historian Karl Lamprecht concluded in a speech held in Dresden in March

Standing Vanguard near Ypres [42]

1915: "What happened here, was German." (*Deutsch ist, was hier geschah.*) [43] Occupation officers hailed the newly Flemishised University of Ghent (jewel in the crown of *Flamenpolitik*) as a German watch-tower and a bulwark against the Latin onslaught. [44] The German presence in Belgium thus acquired a resounding *raison-d'être*: it was transvalued into a resolute vanguard stand for the defence of the Germanic.

As far as Belgium's *raison-d'être* was concerned, proof was once more given that mere agreements did not constitute reality, that deeper truths lurked underneath the *theatrum mundi* of international law. German 'Flanders rhetoric' claimed to uncover the essential phoniness of Belgium, including its defence of its independence in 1914. One widely read Flemish expert, Franz Fromme, called the Belgian resistance against Germany in 1914 a mere bout of hysteria; the unity of Belgians was necessarily shallow and ephemeral, for Belgium was in essence a "hodgepodge" (Fromme used the term *Tohuwabohu*; a fellow expert preferred "Potpourrinia").[45] Belgium, Fromme argued, was in essence the locus of clash between Romance and Germanic and between British and Continental civilisations and those Germans still expressing scruples over the attack on Belgium's independence were ignoring this deep truth at their own peril. (In all its coarseness Fromme's point harks back to the Hegelian notion of struggle as the ultimate reality.)

In short: that which, in the British discourse, had been Belgium's fundamental *raison-d'être*, and that which elevated the defence of Belgium into a matter of principle – namely, the fact that the country owed its independent existence to an international agreement – became, in the German discourse, proof of the country's utter irrelevance – it was, as Sombart had said, "stillborn". Gone at that point was the liberal notion that all civilisations are by definition 'artificial'.

The Flemish rhetoric, it may be observed, carried overtones of ethnic (or, to be more precise, *völkisch*) reasoning. Lamprecht, who before the war had praised Belgium as a microcosm of Europe, now went the way of (what critics called) *Flamenromantik* in his praise of tall blond Flemings' German-ness, and his observations on the short dark Walloons whose hook-nosed, bossy wives were so patently un-Germanic.[46] Meanwhile, those German academics who had the temerity to voice scepticism towards this *Flamenromantik*, faced professional obstruction: one example is the liberal historian Veit Valentin, the other, the socialist historian Gustav Mayer. It is not perhaps a coincidence that both men were to leave Germany in 1933 and both died in exile – Valentin in Washington, Mayer in London. It is not perhaps a coincidence that the Flamenpolitik was largely given shape by men with distinctly authoritarian views, who adhered to a vision of citizens and the state that had strong 'biological' overtones; such as the philologist Herman Wirth, who was during the war a driving force of *Flamenpolitik*, and in 1935 co-founder of the SS-*Ahnenerbe*.

It is true that one should not push the notion of German specificity too far – all of the belligerent nations, without exception, used the language of race. Even the British discourse on Belgium could on occasion be heard to refer to the Belgians as a 'fine race' with the note of approval usually reserved for hunting-hounds. For all that, though, what the Belgian historian Henri Pirenne called the 'zoological' outlook had made the greatest inroads upon German rhetoric. [47]

By way of conclusion

R aymond Aron once defined the difference between both world wars in these terms: whereas the First World War had been about hegemony – in other words, about nationalism – the Second was about ideology. (In other words, only the second conflict made sense.) As John Horne has pointed out, that is a simplification: "both [wars] were about both." [48] World War One was fought by the Entente in the name of the rule of law; and for all the bombast, embroidery, and occasional outright hypocrisy involved, this position cannot be reduced to mere cant. Opponents of liberalism certainly established the link between it and the cause of the Entente. As Mussolini wrote in 1932, "The 'Liberal' century, after having accumulated an infinity of Gordian knots, tries to untie them by the hecatomb of the World War. Never before has any religion imposed such a cruel sacrifice. Were the gods of Liberalism thirsty for blood?"[49]

One dimension of difference with the Second World War is that ideologies were, in nineteenth-century fashion, imagined in national guise. Nations, unquestioningly imagined as group-persons, emblematically, indeed allegorically, carried the weight of entire value-systems. Belgium, as elevated into an emblem of embattled liberalism in British discourse, was a case in point, and one of the last states to ever be so allegorically represented – if not indeed *the* last. This type of anthropomorphism, a form of nineteenth-century naïveté, became, as so many nineteenth-century naïvetés, a casualty of the trenches; and so did, for better or worse, the notion that there could or ought to be such a thing as 'Gallant Little Belgium'.

1   The title of the colloquium at Trinity College Dublin where this contribution was first presented.

2   Konstantin Paustovskii, *The Story of A Life*, Part II: *Restless Youth* (New York, 1967), 264.

3   On the divergent *Weltanschauungen* of Germany and Britain in 1914-1918 and the prewar period, see Modris Eksteins, *Rites of Spring: the Great War and the Birth of the Modern Age* (London/New York, 1989).

4   See excerpt in Joyce Marrow, ed., *The Virago Book of Women and the Great War* (London, 1999), 23.

5   See the humorous verse in Punch magazine, quoted in Barbara Tuchman, *The Guns of August* [1962] (New York, 1994), 92.

6   Quoted in Chrisje and Kees Brants, *Velden van weleer: reisgids naar de Eerste Wereldoorlog* (Amsterdam, 1993), 53.

7   See http://www.ww1-propaganda-cards.com

8   Quoted in Lothar Wieland, *Belgien 1914. Die Frage des Belgischen 'Franktireurkrieges' und die deutsche öffentliche Meining von 1914 bis 1936* (Frankfurt am Main/Bern/New York, 1984), 43.

9   See Gerd Krumeich's entry on 'Einkreisung' (encirclement) in Gerhard Hirschfeld, Gerd Krumeich & Irina Renz, *Enzyklopädie Erster Weltkrieg* (Paderborn, 2003), 452-453.

10 Wilhelm Muehlon, *Die Verheerung Europas. Aufzeichnungen aus den ersten Kriegsmonaten* (Zürich, 1918), 29.

11 See http://www.firstworldwar.com/posters/uk.htm

12 Members of the Oxford Faculty of Modern History, *Why We Are At War: Great Britain's Case* (Oxford, 1914), 115-116. Profits from the sale of this pamphlet went to the *Belgian Relief Fund* and to the badly battered university of Leuven.

13 Eksteins, 77.

14 See, e.g., Wolfgang Mommsen, 'German artists, writers and intellectuals and the meaning of war, 1914-1918', in John Horne, ed., *State, Society and Mobilization in Europe during the First World War* (Cambridge, 1997), 21-38.

15 The point regarding Tennyson is made by the historian Correlli Barnett; see http://www.uea.ac.uk/edu/learn/braysher/charge.htm.

16 *King Albert's Book: A Tribute to the Belgian King and People from Representative Men and Women Throughout the World* (London, 1914), 70.

17 A work by the famous artist Walter Crane, from *King Albert's Book*, 119.

18 *Berliner Tageblatt*, November 2, 1914; quoted in Emile Waxweiler, *La Belgique neutre et loyale* (Paris-Lausanne, 1915), 105.

19 On these massacres, the circumstances in which they occurred, explanations for such violence, and the long and convoluted afterstory, I refer to the by now classic study of John Horne & Alan Kramer, *German Atrocities 1914: A History of Denial* (New Haven/London, 2001).

20 In Walther Stein, *Um Vaterland und Freiheit. Wirklichkeitsaufnahmen aus dem grossen Krieg nebst einer Einführung* (Siegen-Leipzig, 2nd. ed., 1915), Vol. I, 52. To be noted: the attack depicted here is on a German ambulance.

21 Thomas Mann, 'Gedanken Im Kriege', written in August/September 1914; reprint in id., *Essays*, Vol. 1: *Frühlingssturm 1893-1918* (Frankfurt, 1993), 198. See also Mann on the October 1915 execution of Edith Cavell in an essay that pits the 'heroic' against the 'humanitarian': *Betrachtungen eines Unpolitischen*, reprint in id., *Gesammelte Werke* (Oldenburg, 1960), Vol. 12, 444.

22 Jürgen von Ungern-Sternberg and Wolfgang von Ungern-Sternberg, *Der Aufruf 'An die Kulturwelt!' Das Manifest der 93 und die Anfänge der Kriegspropaganda im Ersten Weltkrieg* (Stuttgart, 1996), 163. (I quote the English version as it was published in 1914.)

23 Ibid., 159. (This paragraph did not appear in the English translation.)

24 See the magisterial study of mass delusion, written during the war by the Belgian sociologist Fernand Vanlangenhove, *Comment naît un cycle de légendes. Francs-tireurs et atrocités en Belgique* (Lausanne-Paris, 1916), 31-32, 34-36, 38, 54-67, 78, 80-86, 90-92.

25 Horne & Kramer, 138.

26 Quoted in Horne & Kramer, 156. A chilling comparison, given the German colonial state's 1904-1907 genocidal campaign against the Herero.

27 Van Langenhove, 216-222.

28 Wieland, 55.

29 Stein, 53, ill. 56. On this punitive logic, see John Horne & Alan Kramer, 'German "Atrocities" and Franco-German opinion, 1914: the evidence of German soldiers' diaries', *Journal of Modern History*

66:1 (March, 1994), 1-33. For a striking example, see the propaganda postcard published in Stuttgart entitled "Ein Teufelsbraten", showing a group of Belgian franc-tireurs about to be roasted by the Devil, with accompanying verse calling them "worthless scum". (http://www.ww1-propaganda-cards.com)

30 *Why We Are At War*, 114.

31 Trevor Wilson, *The Myriad Faces of War: Britain and the Great War, 1914-1918* (Cambridge, 1986), 190.

32 In October 1917, Brand Whitlock, the former U.S. envoy, wrote to his literary agent that "the worst that happened there was not the rape of women in Belgium, it was the rape of Belgium." Allan Nevins, ed., *The Letters and Journal of Brand Whitlock*, Part II: The Letters (New York/London, 1936), 237.

33 A point made by the historian E.H. Carr in *The Twenty Years' Crisis, 1919-1939. An Introduction to the Study of International Relations* [1939] (New York, 1964).

34 From the novelist Hall Caine's introduction to *King Albert's Book*, 5.

35 Louis Raemaekers (1869-1956), Dutch-Belgian cartoonist for the Dutch daily *De Telegraaf*; this cartoon is taken from the volume *Het Toppunt der Beschaving*, Fourth Series (The Hague, 1915), but widely published elsewhere. Raemaekers' war drawings had enormous impact in Britain and the U.S.

36 Robert Graves, *Goodbye to all that* [1929] (London, 1960), 153.

37 Lyn MacDonald, *Somme 1916* (London, 1983), 199-200.

38 Wilson, 746, see also 396.

39 On this issue, see Lode Wils, *Flamenpolitik en aktivisme* (Leuven, 1974), confirmed by Winfried Dolderer, *Deutscher Imperialismus und belgischer Nationalitätenkonflikt* (Melsungen, 1989). See also Ulrich Tiedau, 'De Duitse cultuurpolitiek in België tijdens de Eerste Wereldoorlog', in *Bijdragen tot de Eigentijdse Geschiedenis* 11 (2003), 21-45, Frank Wende, *Die belgische Frage in der deutschen Politik des Ersten Weltkrieges* (Hamburg, 1969), and Sophie de Schaepdrijver, 'Occupation, Propaganda, and the Idea of Belgium' in Aviel Roshwald and Richard Stites, eds., *European Culture in the Great War* (Cambridge, 1999), 267-294.

40 Quoted in Lode Wils, *Honderd jaar Vlaamse beweging*, Vol. II (Leuven, 2nd. ed., 1985), 29.

41 Quoted in Wende, 93.

42 In Stein, Vol. 2, 43, Illustration 46.

43 Karl Lamprecht, *Deutsche Zukunft – Belgien. Aus den nachgelassenen Schriften* (Gotha, 1916), 52.

44 Quoted in Karel De Clerck et al., *Kroniek van de strijd voor de vernederlandsing van de Gentse universiteit* (Antwerp, 1980), 117.

45 Fromme's articles in the *Deutsche Rundschau* were collected under the title *Belgisches und Unbelgisches* (Berlin, 1917); Pius Dirr, *Belgien als französische Ostmark* (Berlin, 1917).

46 Lamprecht, *loc. cit.* Female imperiousness had been considered a fundamentally non-German trait at least since Heinrich von Treitschke (see his *Politik*, 3d ed., Leipzig 1913, Vol. I, 244, on the masculine traits of Frenchwomen).

47 In *La nation belge et l'Allemagne* (Ghent, 1920), 15-16. On Imperial attempts to impose a 'racial' perspective on the recalcitrant inhabitants of Alsace-Lorraine, see Alan Kramer, 'Wackes at War: Alsace-Lorraine and the failure of German national mobilization', in John Horne, ed., *State, Society and Mobilization*, 105-121, esp. 120.

48 'Introduction: Mobilizing for 'total war', 1914-1918', in id., ed., *State, Society and Mobilization*, 17.

49 Benito Mussolini, 'The Doctrine of Fascism,' [Enciclopedia Italiana 1932], in Michael Oakeshott, ed. and transl., *The Social and Political Doctrines of Contemporary Europe* (Cambridge UP, 1947), 164-179.

GEERT VAN ISTENDAEL

In Brussels the Word Language Has No Singular

Talking about Brussels is talking about languages. Talking about languages is talking about power. Relationships between languages are never innocent. There's always a certain amount of arm twisting. Strong and weak. High and low. Rich and poor. Centre and periphery. In short, power.

First, let's get the facts straight, simple facts well-known, simple facts not so well-known.

Brussels, a city of one million, the capital of the kingdom of Belgium, more or less the capital of the European Union.

Brussels is an autonomous region with its own regional parliament and its own regional government. The Brussels region is composed of nineteen autonomous municipalities, the city of Brussels itself being only one of these nineteen.

According to Belgian legislation, Brussels is completely bilingual: French/Dutch. *Not* Flemish. Dutch. Flemish people speak all kinds of Dutch like Walloons speak all kinds of French, exactly like people from Québec speak French, and Austrians speak German and also like most Irish people speak English (their brogue being, of course, Irish). In Belgium, you have at least a dozen very different brogues.

So far, so good. Now, prepare yourselves to swallow a couple of facts which are a trifle more complicated. Perhaps a rather elaborate exercise may help you.

When you go to Brussels, take the underground 1B, from the first station Stokkel to, say, a station called *Etangs Noirs/Zwarte Vijvers*, which means more or less Blackwaters, or a little farther to an underground station called Jacques Brel. Now, count the languages you hear, from the very beginning of your trip to the very end. I advise you to use a pencil and a bloc note, because your fingers and toes alone won't do.

First you hear the usual French and Dutch in different colours and variations. Immediately, you will also hear euro-German, euro-Spanish and all thinkable brands of euro-English. Perhaps you'll recognise the hissing sounds of some Slav languages, but mind you, by no means only Polish. Please continue your subterranean trip, but be aware of the fact that, whilst travelling, you are cutting right through a linguistic cross-section in which different languages are neatly juxtaposed exactly like layers in a geological ground profile. Languages underground are always markers of sociological realities at street level. Eurocrat languages in the carriage? This means that, above your head, there are large tree-lined avenues, pleasant, clean parks, huge, elaborate town houses which you would call Victorian, but, of course, they aren't, because we didn't enjoy the reign of that queen.

After the underground station Schuman, under Schuman Square, this deep-frozen and horribly hideous heart of the European Union, you will notice more Belgian sounds than before. But this phenomenon doesn't last. In a couple of minutes, we will already be past the neighbourhood where the offices of the Belgian ministries are located. You will see less

Belgians, you will hear less Belgian dialects. *Etangs Noirs/Zwarte Vijvers/* Blackwaters is not far now. Above your heads, the slums. Garbage. Holes in the pavement. Dire poverty. Voices are now emerging from the depths of throats, raucous, hoarse, guttural. Working class Spanish, a touch of proletarian Portuguese, Arabic, Berber. Albanian perhaps. No Turkish, that's for another underground line, under different rows of slums. The number of languages you can't classify at all is growing rapidly.

The other day, my wife and I were in the underground going home. We were talking about a man called Simon, a nephew of mine. Two boys, I supposed they were North Africans, but I was wrong, were listening to us attentively. One of them asked very politely in very good French:

- *Excuse me, Sir, but this Simon you are talking about, is he perhaps Simon Peter, you know, the apostle?*
- No, I said, he's is just family. He's my nephew.
- *I ask this because we are Christians, Sir,* he replied.

Oh my dear, I thought, are Muslims being converted by Jehova's witnesses these days?

- There are many Christians in this country, I said, in a matter of fact way.
- *Yes, but we are Assyrian Christians,* the other boy cried, *we speak Aramaic, the language of Jesus Christ himself! We speak God's own language!*

We were quite reassured, my wife and I. When the end will be near, Brussels will certainly be saved, because in this, my debauched city, a couple of God fearing boys will be praying at God's feet in God's own language.

The dark skinned boys and girls who are the future of Europe's capital, also paint our traditional national languages with fresh colours. But the French they speak has only a tiny bit in common with the French of

France. The way they speak Dutch is not at all the way other Mediterraneans who emigrated to Holland speak Dutch. Languages in Brussels are prone to multiply themselves. It is as if languages in Brussels' large, unmade, dirty bedstead are constantly copulating in a voluptuous frenzy. Or else, as I put it in one of my poems, here in a free translation by myself:

Brussels is a highly productive language machine
Only young magicians are able to handle it properly

In Brussels, every day again, thousands of people speak dozens of languages they have not really mastered. They pick up a few words and a few idioms, they mix them with a couple of elements they remember from their own, half forgotten mother tongues and they are constantly surfing from one language to another. That's the way people speak in Brussels, the plumber and the butcher, but also the teacher and the politician and even the eurocrat does not escape.

A couple of years ago, I met with a dozen of friends, Flemish and Francophone, in a well-known restaurant, *la Temptation*, to discuss urban problems. No tiresome language issues this time, no, nothing of the kind. We would speak about public transport, council housing, slum problems, refuse collection, air pollution, cars in the city, and so on. After a couple of minutes, however, we discovered that none of the Francophones around the table, not a single one, was a native French speaker. All those Francophones were Belgians, no eurocrats among them, but one had spoken Italian with his parents, another Yiddish, a third one Berber or Arabic or Turkish or Greek etc. etc. This is what Brussels is about today.

Thirty percent of the Brussels population is foreign. When you count those who have Belgian passports but who are clearly first generation Belgians of foreign origin, fifty percent is not far away. The majority of foreigners living in Brussels are, as you might expect, Europeans, but they are not, as you might also expect, working for the European Union or for lobbies trying to influence European decision-making or for companies which decided that they should have a branch in Europe's capital. The large majority of European foreigners are not that kind of people, on the contrary. Most European foreigners are of working class origin. Those people were imported first from Italy, later from Spain, Portugal, Greece and Kosovo, just after the Second World War and down in the fifties and sixties as cheap labour. They stayed in Belgium with their children and their grandchildren. Many of those younger generations have become middle class nowadays, but most of them are not stinking rich at all. The latest wave of cheap European labour is coming, of course, from Poland. And it doesn't stop there. Other waves of immigrants are announced, e.g., from Romania.

In the 1960s and 1970s, official Belgian agents were actively recruiting cheap labour in remote rural areas just outside Europe, first in Morocco, later in Turkey. Today more than ten percent of the Brussels population is Moroccan or of immediate Moroccan origin, about four percent is Turkish or of Turkish origin. Some streets, e.g., *chaussée d'Haecht/ Haachtsesteenweg*, seem to be made up completely of Turkish restaurants. Another street, *rue de Brabant/Brabantstraat*, has developed into a kind of soukh or bazaar where North African and Turkish immigrants from all over Europe are flooding to because this is the place where you find the goodies they can't find elsewhere in Europe and, simply, because it is the place to be for them. Some other neighbourhoods, like Molenbeek, around this underground station *Etangs Noirs/Zwarte Vijvers/*Blackwaters, used to be predominantly working class and Flemish years ago but today they are predominantly Moroccan – and still working class.

My wife grew up in Molenbeek. Only recently, she was talking about her youth to a young Moroccan who lived there. He just refused to believe that this elderly lady, who was undoubtedly Flemish and, according to his criteria, very wealthy, had lived once in *his* poverty stricken neighbourhood.

- *We are all Moroccans here,* he said and he added with great self-confidence:
  always have been.

But then my wife started to furnish some details which only someone who was very familiar with the place could know. About the horse market for instance. About some shops which already had disappeared. About the interior of school buildings. This young Moroccan was baffled. His rock solid frame of reference was crumbling rapidly. Suddenly, he realised that history had already started well before his birth and that today is not necessarily like yesterday or tomorrow. As he had a quick mind, he immediately drew the only possible conclusion:

- *You mean, this neighbourhood, Molenbeek, where I live, was Flemish when you were living here! So Molenbeek used to be rich!*

Now, this young, intelligent Moroccan made a very important remark. In his eyes, Flemish equals rich. Only a couple of minutes ago I said that this part of the city used to be Flemish and working class. Working class doesn't exactly mean rich. What the hell is this all about?

In order to make clear the following point, I'm afraid I have to lead you astray into Belgian history for a short while. Ever since the year of its independence, 175 years ago now, two languages are spoken in Belgium. A small majority, always somewhat more than fifty percent, spoke a series of Dutch dialects, Flemish amongst many others, and more than forty percent spoke all kinds of Walloon dialects. Let's say, for the sake of simplicity, Belgians spoke and speak Dutch and French. However, in the beginning, only French was recognised as an official language. French was the only language admitted in politics, in the civil service, in universities and grammar schools, even in the judiciary. French was also the only language of civilised people *all over Belgium,* in Walloon villages and towns, of course, but also in Flemish boroughs and cities. There is a language divide running from west to east right through the country, a borderline which, with one important exception about which I'll come to speak soon, did not move for more than a thousand years. This is the geographical language boundary. To the North, Dutch is spoken, to the South, French. But there used to be, and to a small extent there still is, another language boundary which has been perhaps even more important for Belgian history and which is invisible. It is the social language boundary. In Belgium, the upper class was always separated from the lower classes, not only by money, not only by education, but also *by language.* The upper class spoke French in otherwise completely Flemish places like Bruges, Antwerp, Ghent and many, many others, even in tiny hamlets the earl spoke French and the farmers spoke, well, a Dutch dialect. This French speaking upper class in Flanders despised the popular Dutch language utterly. They used to say: "Those people even don't speak a language. They just growl sounds a civilised person will never understand." Or worse: "*On parle flamand aux animaux et aux domestiques.* You have to speak Flemish to animals and to servants." In that order.

The emancipation of Dutch language in Belgium is a cultural aspect of a class struggle and I am not a Marxist. The Flemish provinces used to be predominantly agricultural and very poor. The Walloon provinces used to be predominantly industrial and wealthy. At least, mine owners and other captains of industry were extremely rich. Miners and factory workers were like everywhere else: poor. Now, in the course of the twentieth century and especially after World War II, Walloon coal mines and steel mills closed down one after the other, whereas a modern and highly technological industry developed in the Flemish provinces, which were closer to deep water. It's a history of industrial decline comparable to what happened in northern England and in the Midlands. Today, Dutch is no longer despised and the language enjoys full rights in the judiciary, the civil service, at all levels of education etc. There is no more discrimination whatsoever. In the Flemish part of Belgium you see more English than French nowadays. French has simply vanished from public life. So far this short excursion into Belgian history.

How does this apply to Brussels?
Brussels is the place in Belgium where the language boundary *did* move. In Brussels a major language shift took place. Until well into the nineteenth and even twentieth century Brussels was overwhelmingly Dutch-speaking, i.e., one brand of Dutch dialects, called *Brabants*, was generally spoken. Today, Brussels is bilingual, Dutch and French have exactly the same rights, but sociologically, French is the predominating language.

By no means Brussels is the only European city that changed its language or one of its languages. Prague, Budapest, almost all Transsylvanian cities, Czernowitz, Helsinki, Vilnius, Klaipeda, Königsberg or, if you prefer, Kaliningrad, Strasbourg, Nice, Rijeka, all cities in the western parts of

Poland. I don't mention Irish towns and cities here, because I don't know the historical evolution of languages in Ireland. Most language shifts were the result of war, bloodshed, forced migrations and large scale butchering. This, of course, was not the case in Brussels. Language problems in Belgium have always been solved with parliamentary, strictly democratic methods and without violence. Terrorism, like in the Basque country or in Northern Ireland, has never made a chance, not even the slightest one.

However, this language shift did take place in Brussels. I'll give you some figures from the 1846 population census, the first census in the new Kingdom of Belgium and, when you take into account the resources available a hundred and sixty years ago, extraordinarily accurate. The government at the time asked one of the founding fathers of statistics, the mathematician Alphonse Quetelet, to organise this first census. Let's take a municipality which today is considered as being one of the most francophone parts of the Brussels region, Woluwe Saint-Lambert/Sint-Lambrechts Woluwe. In 1846, 0.4% of the population spoke French. That figure is well *under* what was found in many Flemish towns and villages at the time. Take another very French speaking area of Brussels, Etterbeek. In 1846, 2.9% spoke French. Anderlecht: 9.6%. Until the First World War, except in two or three isolated areas, well over eighty percent of the population of what is now the Brussels region had a Dutch dialect as their mother tongue. But the administration was completely French and most of the primary schools were French, although only a tiny minority of the pupils spoke French at home. Secondary schools were always French all over the country until 1930. This explains why so many Flemish people in Brussels were bilingual, even a hundred years ago. It must be absolutely clear that language was a matter of class distinction. French was the better language, full stop. *La Revue Pédagogique Belge*, a review dealing with education problems, describes, in 1894, Flemish school children in Brussels as suffering from hunger and clothed in rags. *L'étincelle*, the review of the Socialist teachers' trade union, writes in 1913 that in Brussels primary schools all abnormal children – today, more sophisticated and politically correct terminology is used, like underprivileged or perhaps deprived, but, of course, that means exactly the same – are poor and 85 % of them are Flemish. The trick is to give them a teacher who only speaks French and who doesn't understand his pupils. There is a famous story about this Brussels teacher speaking in French about a steam engine. His pupils thought he was speaking about an apple tree ...

This method was applied until fairly recently, well into the 1960s. Also parents generally thought it was the best method, sorry, the only method, to learn French quickly and to forget all about this ugly dialect of them. My own dear mother and my aunts always taught me: first you learn French. If my parents hadn't moved to Holland, where a job was offered to my father which he couldn't refuse, I would now be a Francophone. I am Flemish by accident. But many more people in Brussels are French-speaking by accident. There is no choice whatsoever involved. What counted was pressure of status, social ascendance, a certain degree of conformity, a desire to be modern and urbane.

The result has been a major language shift. Before, say, the First World War, the overwhelming majority of the population spoke a Dutch dialect in daily life. But this was not visible. The city looked mostly like an ordinary, middle of the road French town. During the twentieth century, large groups started to abandon their mother tongue and adopted French. Waves of foreign immigration complicated this picture. According to the most recent social research, about 50% of the people in Brussels speak only French at home, 10% speak Dutch, 10% speak Dutch and another language and about 30% speak other languages, unspecified.

During the 1960s and the 1970s, many people in Brussels were extremely hostile against everything Flemish. It was the heyday of the aggressively anti-Flemish political party *Front Démocratique des Francophones*. In those years Flemish people who wanted to speak their language in Brussels shops were often treated very rudely: "Go back to your village, you boor. Speak civilised." It was only a hair breadth away from the well-known racist expression: "Speak white." Even public services, though bilinguism is statutory in Brussels since the 1930s, many times flatly refused to speak Dutch to Flemish citizens.

All this has changed beyond recognition. The city not only looks more bilingual than before. You have two completely separate school networks, one French, one Dutch. Dutch schools are highly successful. Many French speaking parents send their children to those schools, because they will learn the other language and French is taught on a very high level too. Perhaps Dutch schools are even too successful. In some classes it is hard to find one single pupil who speaks at least some Dutch at home. Specialised teachers are appointed to deal with this new type of language problem. In public services, town halls, post offices, police stations, etc. language laws are, most of the time, abided by – with only one important exception, an outrageous and shameful exception. Too many hospital doctors in Brussels still refuse to understand what their Flemish patients say. In fact, they are behaving like vets. A cow cannot explain where it hurts.

But otherwise, a new climate is developing rapidly. Perhaps the autonomous status acquired by the Brussels Region in 1989, well after the Flemish and Walloon Regions, is gradually beginning to pay off. Brussels has a regional parliament and a regional government. Of course regional elections are democratic. But please don't jump to conclusions. This doesn't mean that Dutch speakers in Brussels are for ever condemned to the opposition benches. A system of careful checks and balances has been established in order to protect the Dutch speaking minority in Brussels. Legally, the Brussels region cannot be governed *against* one language group. Brussels regional governments *have* to be bilingual on an *equal* basis. An almost equal basis. All acts of regional government have to be published in both languages. All regional public services have to be fully bilingual. When one of the two language groups in the regional parliament deems a measure discriminating, it has the right to block parliamentary procedure. In fact, deputies always try to avoid this. The effect of being forced by law to work together across language barriers can only be called salutary. You try to find solutions to important urban problems such as slum clearance, the protection of monuments, public transportation, traffic jams, waste disposal, petty crime, unemployment, etc., in short, all problems that have nothing to do with language.

Perhaps I forget a little detail: how do you distinguish between language groups? In Brussels regional elections, it is illegal for bilingual parties to participate. So you have two Social-Democratic parties, two Conservative parties, two Christian-Democratic parties and two Green parties. The Flemish Green party just has one single deputy. People are free to vote what they like, of course, but in Brussels this means that Francophones vote Flemish and Flemish people vote Francophone. Inevitably, thousands of people are more or less bilingual. In Brussels the language divide is not a sharp, thin line but a large grey area in between. Many people feel that the language boundary cuts right through their skulls. It is, e.g., an established fact that the extremely nationalist and extreme right wing Flemish party *Vlaams Belang* attracts loads of Francophone voters. Their programme is disgustingly racist.

About fifteen percent of Brussels regional deputies have an Arab surname. One member of region government is of Turkish origin. I think the integration and emancipation of Muslim people has been achieved *only in politics*. I think our political parties from all opinions did a very good job. There is even one deputy of Moroccan origin who belongs to the left wing of the democratic Flemish nationalists. That's what I call full integration.

This does not mean that integration in other fields is already a fact. Not at all. Perhaps you may think that language strife is the most important problem in the bilingual capital of a bilingual kingdom. Again: not at all. Problem number one in Brussels is the integration of large groups of young male Muslims.

Unemployment among them is soaring. They have not acquired adequate schooling. Too many of them leave school without the necessary qualifications. But even with the right degrees and certificates, they are still excluded by many employers. They are heavily over represented in the statistics of unemployment and petty crime. The other half of young Moroccans, I mean the girls and women, are completely different. They are next to absent from the statistics of petty crime, more absent than any other category, e.g., high class Belgian girls, and many of them acquire, sometimes in very difficult circumstances, all degrees you can wish. Many employers exclude them too, but this is changing slowly – too slowly. One of the problems of both young Moroccan girls and boys in Brussels is that many of them are not bilingual French/Dutch. It is next to impossible to find a job in and around Brussels without being more or less bilingual, French/Dutch. Most of those young people visited French speaking schools in Brussels. Dutch is a compulsory subject in these schools, but it has been badly served by teachers in the past. This is changing now, but still Dutch-speaking schools deliver perfectly bilingual eighteen year-olds, whereas the reverse is simply not true.

I think the integration of those young North African – and, to a lesser extent, Turkish – people is the most important problem Brussels has to face in the near future. One Moroccan teacher (of Dutch language and literature) told me the other day that there were three problems facing young Moroccans today and in the nearby future. "Number one", he said, "is work. Number two is work. Number three is work."

There is no large scale spreading of Muslim fundamentalism in Brussels, though some imams are known to praise terrorism and in a few mosques there is some recruiting going on. But all this remains very limited. The trouble is rather that our type of economy is utterly incapable of solving the job problem. We would have to get rid of our obsession with the free market. The market has never really been known to provide full employment. One of our most distinguished university professors, ms. Cantillon – she is of Christian-Democratic persuasion and specialised in problems of social security – has argued that in order to solve the job problem, there is no other way out than to disrupt the free market by creating jobs which yield no profits. Though I entirely agree with Professor Cantillon, I am very pessimistic about the possibilities of pushing Belgian politicians in that direction. And I am even more pessimistic about the European Commission. The European commissioners are real high priests of the golden calf, I mean, of the free market. And they are utterly blind for the disruptive evolution happening under their very eyes, I mean, in Brussels. To me it seems they are not really living in Brussels, but on some planet at the far end of our solar system. The non-integration of the European rich is a major problem but this problem is hardly ever taken seriously by politicians.

Integration by employment, that's the crux of Brussels' future. I'll mention but two other important problems.

There is, what I would call, urban planning. This includes careful planning of public spaces, protection of monuments, an efficient public transportation system, slum clearance and a severe limitation of car access to the city. For years, *Brusselisation* has been a household word among city planners. It meant wholesale destruction of entire areas and afterwards highly profitable office building. The quality of the architecture was totally unimportant. Brussels didn't need the blitz to be destroyed. We did it ourselves, after the war. In Brussels, demolition simply meant progress. The most valuable buildings were pulled down indiscriminately. In the 1890s, Brussels was for a short while the capital of European architecture. It is still considered as the capital of art nouveau (Jugendstil, Modern Style). The most important gem of this type of architecture, *la Maison du Peuple* by Victor Horta, vanished from the earth forty years ago. This devilish self-destruction has now been stopped. Only the European quarter is still eating up its surroundings. Schuman Square, the heart of the European Union, is by far the ugliest square in Europe. But in many other parts of the city, a new type of policy is giving results. After decades the so-called city cancers – houses left to rot by their owners for reasons of speculation – are at last being taken away from irresponsible owners and taken over by public authorities. New life is entering the city everywhere, young families, posh shops, fashionable pubs, little squares are carefully landscaped, after years of dogs turds, graffiti and general neglect. This means a certain degree of gentrification, but this does not mean that only the rich can afford to live in Brussels. It's rather a kind of young middle and lower middle class. According to London, Paris and Dublin standards, housing is still dirt cheap in Brussels, though this is changing too.

Traffic jams are still relatively mild in Brussels, especially when you realise that about three hundred thousand people from all over Belgium commute into the city every day. After years of tiresome discussions, the national railway company is now starting to extend its suburban network considerably. Young and bright politicians are working out measures to limit the free access of cars to the city centre. But too many battles are still fought between the region and the nineteen municipalities which are, in fact, as many fiefs defending fiercely their privileges. Most mayors, not all of them but most, are local boys and their idea of the city can be summed up in two words: "My power and my profit."

Another problem is specific to Brussels: the city cannot extend its limits. It cannot incorporate suburban and freshly urbanised areas. Brussels is a bilingual isle in the Flanders region. It is virtually unthinkable that Flemish politicians will allow bits and pieces of their region to be incorporated into the Brussels region. In some of the villages close to Brussels, 70 or even 80% of the people speak French and they enjoy an efficient and rather elaborate system of protection, the so-called facilities. But they are still considered by Flemish politicians as those rich, bourgeois, upper class people who forced their language on lower class, Flemish villagers. Historically, this is undoubtedly true, though nowadays lots of Flemish people are just as rich as French-speaking people. Anyway, the result is that the economic hinterland of Brussels belongs to another Region with other regulations and legislation and that urban and linguistic realities don't correspond to legal boundaries. To change these boundaries would mean to change compromises which often only have been reached after many years of terribly complicated and never satisfying negotiations. Perhaps it is preferable not to reopen Pandora's box, after all.

I would like to end with a more cheerful note.
If one thing is separated in a federal state like Belgium, it is, of course, culture. We have two ministers of Culture and there is no such thing as a cultural treaty between the Dutch-speaking and the French-speaking Community. What in fact do we see in Brussels today, for somewhat more than a decade now? Artists of all disciplines are eager to work together, regardless of language. More and more initiatives are taken to realise in artistic practice what is impossible in political practice. This is very complicated. You have to negotiate with two administrations, with people who suspect each other of trying to push all kinds of Trojan horses through the well defended gates – in fact, this phrase has been used once by a former minister of French culture: "*Le cheval de Troie flamand*, the Flemish Trojan horse", he said, whatever that may be. Every year, for more than ten years now, the *KunstenfestivalDesArts* is staging avant garde theatre, dance, music, video and what have you from all over the planet, in all kinds of languages, in all kinds of different Brussels theatres. Flemish people go to French theatres they never visited before, they hardly knew they existed. And, of course, vice versa. A highly sophisticated electronic system of supertitling has been developed. You see for instance Chinese comedians playing in Chinese and you read the translation in both national languages at the same time at the top of the stage. In all European

countries, this festival enjoys a reputation as being outstanding. The Paris newspaper *Libération* wrote: *"Désormais, Bruxelles donne l'exemple* (From now on, Brussels sets an example)."* I assure you, when a Paris newspaper writes things like this, something *is* happening outside Paris. Even New York seems to have discovered that a couple of savages are doing something in the woods around Brussels that might be of some interest after all. More recently, a bilingual House of Literature has opened its doors downtown. It is called: *Passa Porta.* Come through the doors. Forget about passports. The reference is crystal clear. Writers come to read in Estonian, German, French, Dutch, Spanish, Arabic, Hebrew (together, those two) and even in English. The public is a complete mix of Brussels cultures. Young, old, poor, rich, everybody who is interested in prose or poetry tries to be there.

When culture becomes a dynamic force, be it only in a small part of the city, when culture breaks through old prejudices and separations, when culture brings together very different people in respect of their differences, I think there is some hope. In this respect, Brussels, because of its historic multiplicity is a privileged place. Maybe one day, Brussels could become a real capital of Europe. I didn't say of the European Union, but of Europe, that is, of a humanistic, polyglot, polycentric, open and compassionate society.

BENNO BARNARD

Belgium's Culture: A Dutchman's view

The citizens of today's Europe are all provincials, particularly those who speak a non-international language. And it is my prediction that within a generation or so all fifty or sixty languages currently spoken in Europe will be regarded as regional, at least inside Europe, with the exception of English, whether we like those dyspeptic British tea-drinkers or not.

Now here's a sharp distinction between the Irish and the Belgians among us. I vividly remember ordering a glass of beer in an Irish pub in Leuven some years ago, a stone's throw away from a university founded in the fifteenth century. The barmaid turned out not to speak a word of Dutch, and it became clear that she believed I belonged to some alien species, not at home in this world. "This is an Irish bar," she crowed. "Why is it," I replied,"that you treat me exactly the same way as the English used to treat your ancestors?"

The only ones interested in the Dutch-speaking cultural world, or worlds, are other small cultures, for they know what it means to be small: the sole chance of a successful cultural exchange is the mutual awareness of belonging to a dwarf nation. Rather misunderstood by the Balkans than taunted by an English-speaking barmaid. "We have to be Flemings in order to become Europeans", is another battle cry rising from Flemish history: one has to be a provincial in order to become a European.

There are at least some fifty Europes, and that is precisely what consti-
tutes Europe. Between all those Europes we need an exchange of as many
literary works, films and plays as possible, taking into account that works
of art require a certain provincialism in order to be universal. Every half-
educated European is familiar with the crucial moments of German history in the twentieth century, but what makes *Heimat* such a masterpiece
is its focus on the local, the provincial, the Schabbechian.

From a Dutch/Flemish perspective there's quite some irony in the
thought that Germany and France are well on their way to becoming
small nations too, linguistically speaking. Dutch/Flemish literature is
widely translated into German and French nowadays, not into English.
Many English-speaking Europeans – present company excluded, of course
– wallow in their linguistic greatness, the Empire now consisting of words
instead of colonies. I would like to remonstrate against that attitude, con-
tending that much English-language cosmopolitanism is in fact a
dressed-up form of provincialism.

To my mind the best method of creating cosmopolitanism is swapping
various forms of provincialism. But the problem of texts is that they don't
always travel from one province to another that easily. Music, ballet,
paintings, sculptures, they all travel well, the language of notes and
images being fairly universal in the western world. But literature often
wants all kinds of footnotes explaining allusions, names, historical facts
and the like, to readers who did not grow up in the same cultural and historical environment as the author. Even the Netherlands and Flanders,
two swamps divided by one language, sometimes need explanatory
notes for each other's texts. In a theatre monologue of my hand, *A Public
Woman*, the actress remembers the marital guide of a Catholic nature

which was always on her parents' bedside table, *Le marriage parfait* (*The Perfect Marriage*); but when the play was performed in Amsterdam, it turned out that many spectators didn't understand that French title. Apparently, I have become too Flemish, having spent nearly three decades in Flanders.

Have I?

Let me first correct that definition of me as 'a Dutchman in Flanders'. If anything, I'm a Dutchman in *Belgium*, a country by the North Sea with a view of the Mediterranean world, thanks to its bilingualism. In many ways Belgium *is* Europe, and I believe today offers an appropriate occasion to paraphrase a well-known French saying: "*Chaque homme a deux patries, la sienne et la Belgique.*" (*Every man has two home countries, his own and Belgium.*)

I cherish the gentle multicultural chaos Belgium has to offer. Belgium is like everybody's mistress, generously holding up her breasts to every intelligent man who happens to come by. I'm very grateful that by a mere fluke I did not end up as a Dutch writer living in Amsterdam, speaking a throaty form of my mother tongue, and with some notions of only one foreign language: English. For the Flemish it's an article of faith that a Dutchman who speaks any French at all must speak Voltaire's language abominably, with an accent thick enough to knock out a bull; but I have Belgium to thank for my rather acceptable knowledge of French.

My half-educated European who's familiar with the crucial moments of German history in the past century, is also supposed to be aware of Flanders' historically awkward relationship with the French language. Nowadays, the Flemish struggle for cultural and linguistic autonomy is water under the bridge; what remains is the advantage of the Latin proximity four million French-speaking Belgians embody. The elderly generation in Flanders became familiar with the intricacies of French grammar under duress: linguistic oppression provided them with the key to Enlightenment, and in general to a broader horizon than their own parochial little world's outlook.

But now that the battle for Flemish emancipation has been fought, now that the Flemings have prevailed, now the leaders of the various nationalist movements, carefully cultivating their inherited traumas, are chucking in the bin the very knowledge that gave their people an intellectual edge on the Dutch: the knowledge of French.

Recently Bart De Wever, the chairman of a rather right-wing but democratic Flemish-nationalist party, bumptiously stated in the daily *De Standaard* that his French was far from perfect; and on television he told a French-speaking journalist that he demanded to be interviewed in *Flemish*. In Flanders, saying you speak Flemish instead of *Dutch*, the language former generations of intellectuals made every effort to speak, equals saying you prefer dialect to the civilised form of your mother tongue, the form which enables you to communicate with twenty million people.

Modern Flemish nationalism, nagging for a Flemish army and Flemish stamps, seem to be a good way to ruin a nice country. But on top of the problem the Flemish nationalists have with their French-speaking compatriots, they also seem to be tangling with their northern fellow-speakers of Dutch; in that perspective Mr. De Wevers desire to speak "Flemish" may well have been a Freudian slip.

Historically, a Dutchman in Belgium pretty much resembles an Englishman in Ireland, with this crucial distinction that the Dutch were masters in Belgium for no longer than fifteen years, during the period 1815-1830. Also, they caused no potato famine. Now that I come to think of it, the analogy is historically false: the Flemish could speak their own language under the regime of King William I, and Dutch was not imposed on the Walloons. The only likeness between Flanders and Ireland is the fact that Dutch (respectively English) spoken with a Dutch (respectively English) accent is often met with irony, and sometimes with distrust or even irritation.

The Dutch are generally abhorred in Flanders, particularly but not exclusively among the less educated. They are regarded as unrefined, rude, loud, and impervious to subtleties – rather in the style of Erasmus, who mocked them as mental pachyderms. Erasmus by the way was a Dutchman who lived in Brussels for a while.

For the past thirty years, ever since I moved to Belgium in 1976, I've experienced what it feels like to be treated as a foreigner. My dearest friends are Belgians, but all the same I'm regularly the target of a verbal manifestation of xenophobia; a snowball pelted at my brainpan. Often enough the remark as such is completely innocent: "Hey, you Dutchman!" But sometimes the snowball contains a stone and my nut starts bleeding. In my case it concerns the dislike of someone who has tried to really integrate, up to the point of allowing himself an opinion of his own about this country. Oh yes, I'm very welcome – provided I only say kind and grateful things.

Consequently, I don't have too much confidence in the tolerance of that virtual Flemish republic, so ardently craved by the various nationalist movements, factions and parties, and to be formed from a region which is already so right-wing that the Liberal-Conservative party seems to be left-wing by contrast. The ideology of national purity threatens to dominate us more and more, and therefore I say: "*La patrie n'est pas une idée fausse, mais elle est une idée petite qui doit rester petite.*"(*The fatherland is not a wrong idea, but it is a small idea that must remain so*).

Which basically means that I'm in favour of Belgium.

MARC REYNEBEAU

Belgian Quixotry
Historiography and society in the quest
for consensus

The knowns and the unknowns

Every country has its own dirty little secrets – *raison d'état oblige* – and Belgium is certainly no exception to that. Sometimes they surface after a period of time, sometimes they linger in obscurity forever and become the "unknown unknowns", as the US Secretary of Defence Donald Rumsfeld coined the phenomenon: the facts of which we don't know that we don't know them. But a secret is not always what it seems to be. Often it turns out that what is considered to be hidden history or a concealed fact, is merely an ignored or forgotten one. After all, answers only come as a reply to a question.

It is the historian's task to reactivate fading memories, to dig up the buried past and to blow the dust of long established so-called historical truths. Historians should never forget that the truth is a value with an expiry date. Historical truth can only be established for a limited period of time. The past can always do with some re-examination, which makes revisionism a historiographer's virtue. History is the craft of endless rewriting, of continuous reconsideration of the facts as they are (or were). Every new generation has its own questions to ask, its own criteria to define relevance and its own language in which it prefers history to be told.

To be honest, the Belgian establishment of academic historians is seldom to be found in the forward trenches of historical re-examination. Certainly, this historiographic elite is internationally rather well-renowned, but this relates to its methodological prowess and its high technical standards in developing auxiliary sciences rather than to imaginative power, moral courage to embark on a daring journey of full-fledged revisionism or tackle new issues and sensitive subjects.

Controversy is usually no impetus for historical research. This is an empirical fact, not a natural law. For a long time academic historiography in Belgium tended to shy away from controversial issues in Belgium's (recent) past, e.g., the early colonisation of Central Africa, Belgium's involvement in postcolonial Congo, the attitude of certain groups and individuals during Second World War, or the so-called Royal Question when King Leopold III stood at the centre of a political storm because of his much disputed behaviour during World War II.

A critic should be critical towards himself as well. So it is important to note that these examples of neglected historical topics have a common denominator: the monarchy. Even when the subject ostensibly refers to the colony, there too, in fact, disputed actions of kings (in the Congo) are the main issue. Why is that? Is it because these really are the *only* so-called sensitive issues? Or is it because they are the first to come to mind, as the monarchy is a symbolically important, popular and high profiled institution? Maybe the critic is tempted by some sensationalism?

The ambiguities of forgetting

Indeed it is not difficult to find examples of other highly relevant issues which rarely catch the attention of the scholarly community. Consider the social system, for instance, which was developed in the Belgian Congo during the 1950s and which very much resembled apartheid, or the one-sidedness of the economic historiography on the nineteenth century (see *infra*), or the Brabant Revolution of the late eighteenth century which is largely ignored, although it became a symbolically important reference for the Belgian revolution of 1830.

Another striking example is the agrarian crisis in Flanders in the 1840s, a human catastrophe that bears some resemblance to the Great Famine in Ireland. In handbooks or historical overviews the crisis is usually treated more or less as an anecdote – yes, we know that life was bad in the nineteenth century – or merely as an illustration of a major shift in economic history: the decline of domestic labour by farmers who could no longer compete with the mechanised textile industry.

Theoretically this tragedy could have been used as a political argument, as it was (and still is) in Ireland. Of course, the Belgian establishment of the time was not very interested as it was not concerned with anything that lay beyond its own interests. After all, it thought that progress required the sacrifice of the traditional agricultural sector to the more profitable industrialisation. Despite some important monographic studies the overall historiographic neglect of the crisis apparently sipped through in mainstream historiography. This was not corrected later on.

Theoretically again this correction could have been in the making as a result of Belgium's federalisation process, which gave the Flemish Community authority over, among other competences, education and scientific research. In a simple and well-known nationalistic rhetoric the horrors of the past could have been used as a justification and legitimisation for the new Flemish autonomy. This did not happen. The image of a miserable past seemed incompatible with what today's wealthy Flanders wants to remember: not a story of failures and misery, but a succession of successes.

A single exception in this pattern of selective official memory is the public attention given – for a while at least – to Daensism, a late nineteenth century Catholic social movement with *flamingant* leanings in a small Flemish industrial city.[1] It certainly is no coincidence that Catholicism and flamingantism are classic *topoi* of conservatism in Flanders. And in the end, the new Flemish leadership is only slightly less elitist than the Belgian establishment it replaced. Moreover, this new elite is largely driven by a free market logic (for instance, in the late twentieth century it very intensely promoted a 'third industrial revolution'), in which there can be no mercy for uncompetitive economic activities, not now, not in the past. Sorry about that.

Amnesia's sideshow

Some subjects are 'forgotten' because they are unsuitable for present-day political goals. On other issues outdated historical images still linger in the collective memory because they were not sufficiently corrected by 'revisionist' historical research. This is the case for the economic historiography on the nineteenth century which is still marred by an elitist view that does not link industrial successes to low wage social policies, including the absence of compulsory education.

Another example is the well-known and occasionally still used expression, the 'coup of Loppem', which defines an important meeting of King Albert with Belgian political leaders in the immediate aftermath of World War I. But it is important to keep in mind that the expression stands for a very particular interpretation of what happened during that meeting. To be more precise, it claims that, under the Socialist threat of a Soviet-style revolution, the King was blackmailed into accepting general suffrage. In hindsight then the expression is nothing more than the reflection of the anger of Catholic conservatives who did not accepted the one man-one vote system and therefore defined its introduction as a *coup d'état*: a coup against the authority they wanted to maintain.

The Dutch (Flemish) phrase "keizer-koster" ("emperor-sexton") equally illustrates the phenomenon of outdated historical labels which, uncorrected, linger on. The phrase is used pejoratively to describe a busybody. On average about once a month a politician is called an 'emperor-sexton', especially when (s)he tries to regulate this or that sector of public life. Probably few users of the phrase know that it originates in the rhetoric attacks on the Habsburg monarch Joseph II, who ruled the Southern Netherlands (today's Belgium, more or less) in the late eighteenth century. In his attempt to modernise the country's very archaic institutions he collided with the then very powerful Catholic Church by threatening its ideological, fiscal and other privileges and monopolies. Hence labelling him a meddler reflects a very biased and more specifically clerical representation of history.

The lack of authoritative historical research on certain subjects may have other consequences. Neglected social groups start writing their own history if they think their contribution to society is not fully acknowledged by academic historiography – or if that does not serve their political ambitions. But of course, if they do so, they do it on their terms, from their own particular, necessarily partisan perspective. A classic example is social history, which was largely developed by left wing and socialist historians. An even more striking example is the history of the Flemish Movement: especially after World War II (when a number of organisations within the Flemish Movement collaborated with the Germans) it was considered unpatriotic and thus unworthy of serious academic effort. As a result Flemish nationalism, for a long time, was able to monopolise its own history.

As these movements solitarily constructed their own historic tradition – and the same goes for feminists, ecologists, ethnic and other minorities, pressure groups etc. – they claim the territory as their own and only reluctantly accept 'intrusions' from critical outsiders who challenge their historical dogmas and their sometimes hagiographic or teleological historiography. The necessary deconstruction of the widespread mythography is often considered to be pure muckraking. Then an ownership debate arises: who owns this particular slice of history? Who has the right to write about it? Does the would-be student really need to be part of the in-group? Nowadays this phenomenon is clearly visible in the debate on Belgian colonial history. Fearing a negative historical judgment, associations of former 'colonials' in the Congo often implicitly state that one had to have been 'there' fully to understand the colonial era, including the 'negro mentality', the blessings of the civilisation Belgium brought to Africa etc.

Living with outsiders

The limits of historic curiosity and knowledge are never, however, determined by academic zeal or courage or the lack thereof. The absence of academic research on certain controversies created an open playing field – if not for partisan historiography – for non-historians and non-Belgians. Innovative studies on WWII and its aftermath were written by the American John Gillingham, the British historian Martin Conway and the sociologist Luc Huyse. The most revealing research on the Belgian colonisation of Congo was undertaken by the British journalist Neil Ascherson, the American Adam Hochschild, the anthropologist Daniel Vangroenweghe, the diplomat Jules Marchal (E.M. Delathuy) and the sociologist Ludo De Witte. More often than not, the academic establishment has dismissed these authors as being biased or sensationalist or lacking in academic rigour. Or it simply ignored their findings.

Not only academics react with disdain and irritation to what is considered an intrusion by outsiders. Politicians do the same when they think that the dissemination of historical knowledge does not suit their (personal) plans. Early 2004 the documentary *White King, Red Rubber, Black Death* by the British film maker Peter Bate on the horrors of King Leopold II's exploitation regime in Congo was broadcasted on the BBC and scheduled to be shown on Belgian television. The then Belgian minister of Foreign Affairs Louis Michel made a very unusual move by venturing into the realm of historical criticism. He denounced the film as a "tendentious diatribe" and his office published an official refutation. [2]

To be fair, it should be noted that historians were, to say the least, not always encouraged to tackle sensitive issues. When the Royal Question was settled with the abdication of Leopold III in 1950, the politicians involved made an informal agreement not to discuss the matter any longer and not to reveal any information about it. Key figures refused to be interviewed on the subject, archives remained closed. Nevertheless, some protagonists, especially within the royal family, continued to advocate their case in the conflict by selectively releasing documents to certain historians whom they considered trustworthy.[3]

When three decades later a popular television series on Belgium's wartime history brought up the matter again, Leopold III broke his silence for the first time by stating in a letter to the prime minister that all this hullabaloo was unnecessary and that he would continue ... to remain silent. The incident did stimulate him, however, to writing his memoirs. They were only published in 2001, eighteen years after his death in 1983. In this book – in no time a local bestseller – the former King defended his wartime views and suggested that the historians who had described him as being authoritarian were "not impartial". Ironically, Leopold's book unequivocally confirmed the authoritarian political opinions of the King, to which apparently he stuck all his life. But it also made clear that the official secrecy did not hide very much any more.

Quite contrary to the intentions of those responsible for it, the yearlong secrecy had not relegated the conflict to oblivion. It created paranoia. Only this was certain: something was held from the general public. But what could that be? The question provoked all sorts of sometimes grotesque suspicions about the King's wartime past. Alas, they could neither be confirmed nor denied because of the lack of reliable sources.

After a few decades, however, enough information had sipped through to turn the Secret of the Royal Question very much into a historical monster of Loch Ness. It turned out that in the end there wasn't much to it – apart from the fact that Leopold could hardly be considered a staunch supporter of the democratic system. And indeed, this was the core of what the political elite had tried to conceal, for this fact was utterly incompatible with the King's constitutional obligations. A king is not supposed to indulge in partisan political opinions, let alone to express them, especially if they clash with the very essence of the country's political system. After all it is no coincidence that during the German occupation of Belgium Leopold had been brooding on a new constitution inspired by Salazar's dictatorship in Portugal.

Damage control

As the political elite after the war failed to convince the King that he had made a political error – hence the Royal Question – they chose to save the institution by sacrificing the one person jeopardising its existence. The politicians dreaded the risky transformation of Belgium into a republic – and they still do. Institutional and political continuity was the main objective of their thinking. Leopold was forced to step aside in favour of his elder son, the then 20 year-old Prince Baudouin, who after his death in 1993 was succeeded by his brother, the present King Albert II.

In hindsight everything falls into place. In order not to endanger the entire system the political elite believed it simply had to obscure the fact that this one individual, Leopold, refused to play the game by the book. It had done so since 1940, when the King had broken with the political elite, so why shouldn't it continue to do so in 1950 and afterwards? In order to save the monarchy as a widely accepted and vital institution of Belgium's democratic system, the King's real intentions were never to be revealed. Until he did so himself, posthumously, in 2001.

It is strange to realise that all the time that the Royal Question dragged on, the stubborn King's opponents within the elite disposed of some very damaging evidence, mostly incriminating texts written by Leopold III himself. Although this information might have sustained their case very convincingly, they never used it in the public debate. They abstained from sharing the evidence with the population. Although a referendum was held on the matter in 1950 – a unicum in Belgian history – and although the elections of the time were strongly influenced by the controversy, the electorate was never fully aware of what was really at stake.

The political elite refused to make the population its ally and treated it as an outsider, because it did not want to risk loosing its control over the political agenda. The politicians in charge did not want a fundamental public discussion on the ideological base of the state; their only objective was damage control. In terms of political and institutional stability there was more to be gained than lost by not revealing certain facts. Already very early on in the Royal Question the search for stability – a prerequisite for the elite's ability to maintain power – gained the upper hand over democratic transparency.

In all this, serenity was (and still is) the official key word. Serenity defines the civilised way of taking care of business. Serenity must be kept at all times. Discord or dissent must not come in the way of serenity. Facts which might disturb serenity must be kept under the lid. Therefore some issues should not be discussed publicly.

What's the use anyway? Let bygones be bygones. And of course, because it is a sophisticated democracy, Belgium does it the soft way. Historians or journalists are not routinely thrown in jail, they simply are not encouraged to venture on the high seas of political controversy – there is enough to do anyway. And if some foolish student should still tackle controversial issues, it is easy, again, to overlook or ignore his or her research.

Sometimes there is an exception to that rule as some controversial historical research can nevertheless be politically useful. So it is not really an exception after all: it merely confirms the rule of political utility and opportunity. In 2004, Louis Michel did not want too much light be shed on the early years of Belgian presence in the Congo. In 1999, however, and after some hesitation, he welcomed the publication of a rather disturbing book on Belgium's involvement in the murder in 1961 of Patrice Lumumba, the first prime minister of the newly independent Republic of Congo. [4] The minister supported the formation of a parliamentary commission of inquiry on the matter that got access to many sources that were and still are closed to historians. The commission largely confirmed the central thesis of the book.

Michel's attitude can be explained in the context of his extensive diplomatic efforts from 1999 onwards to help to bring peace to war ravaged Central Africa. In these efforts he was driven by a very commendable and idealistic concern for the suffering people in the area. But of course, if he were to succeed in his undertaking, it would equally substantially increase his international diplomatic esteem. A successful peacemaker is highly regarded on the world stage – maybe as a potential Nobel Prize Winner.

Louis Michel's tacit endorsement of the book on Lumumba had to prove that Belgium did not harbour any hidden neo-colonialist agenda – and that the minister was a genuine and trustworthy mediator in the peace talks. The reason behind his dismissal of Peter Bate's film was to deny any suggestion that the colonial rule of King Leopold II was instrumental in the emergence of a culture of violence in Congo – and to protect the monarchy and thus the country from bad press. Apparently, one can criticise certain aspects of Belgian history, but not any royal involvement therein.

Celebrating anniversaries

Serenity refers to the absence of conflict. Belgium cherishes the idea of serenity because intrinsically it is a divided country, characterised by many fault lines. These fault lines are not uncommon to other countries. Belgium, however, has the habit of ignoring them, of playing them down, of not really solving them but of finding ways to dissimulate them in a consensus. Division should never escalate into open conflict. The central reasoning behind this habit is the idea that the country's survival very much depends on its ability to overcome these divisions – or to ignore them. And of course if the basic societal consensus remains unchanged, the stability of the powers that be is guaranteed.

Belgium has a long tradition of compromise, of establishing and maintaining a consensus that tones down political strife. That consensus is essentially an elitist one. In most cases party leaders discreetly try to find their way around controversies, which is most commonly achieved by throwing taxpayers' money at it. The solutions are only approved of *post factum* by the rank and file.

Already in 1830, the founding fathers of the new state cautioned the people with the national motto, "Strength through unity". This was a very blunt acknowledgment of Belgium's division, as it referred to the 'monster coalition' of Catholics and Liberals who had joined forces in the 1820s to oppose the Dutch King William I, under whose crown Belgium and the Netherlands were brought together in 1815. The coalition was 'unnatural' in the sense that it could not, and did not, claim ideological unity; it was pragmatism which made the different parties unite in opposition. Not intentionally but because of the King's stubbornness it evolved into a full blown patriotic movement that led the country to independence. Once Belgium was internationally firmly recognised, the coalition ceased to exist and gave way to a profound and long lasting ideological balancing act which still exists today.

The country's founding years do not generate a great deal of historiographic activity, not in academia nor in the publishing world. In 2005, the year Belgium celebrated its 175th anniversary, only one new book on 1830 was published. It was not written, by the way, by a professional historian, but by a journalist. The previous mass market book on the subject was published exactly a quarter of a century earlier, in 1980, on the occasion of the celebration of 150 years of independence. That one was written by a lawyer. Of course, this makes it very easy to keep up with the literature on the Belgian revolution.

The publication dates are significant: it is only when the country has a birthday to celebrate that a new book on the revolution is worth publishing. And one is enough. As if one sends a birthday card because one has to: not out of affection but merely because it is a social habit to do so.

Belgium's intrinsic division is well illustrated by the fact that official celebrations of the country's independence often turn into an occasion to manifest dissent. In 1855, the still very young Flemish Movement used the celebrations as a forum to protest against the inequity the Dutch language suffered in an officially bilingual but *de facto* French speaking country. In 1880, the Catholics did not participate in the celebrations because the Liberal government of that time intended to put an end to some essential Catholic educational monopolies (the first 'School War'). In 1905, it was the Socialists' turn to protest and highlight their disagreement with the political discrimination against the poor.

Yet it is possible to give a more positive interpretation to this tradition of protest: the festive occasion as forum that *can* be appropriated in order to draw attention to fundamental political issues. The emphasis of this interpretation then lies with the *discursive* strengthening of cohesion and unity. And so the tradition of manifesting dissent on anniversary parties can be appropriated once more, this time to become part of a recuperation process. It is then to celebrate ideological, cultural and linguistic diversity and plurality as fundamental characteristics of the country, as if they were a national asset.

The ambivalence of and the ambiguities in the function of history in the national debate again are clearly visible in the celebrations of the 175th anniversary of Belgium's revolution in 2005. To begin with, officially these were the '175-25' celebrations, the latter figure referring to a quarter century of federalism. This is a little odd because the country's devolution process already started in 1970. 1980 – the year referred to in the '175-25'-logo – already marked its second phase. Moreover, the notion of federalism was only introduced in 1993. So the meaning of the figure '25' is symbolic rather than historic. It refers to the way in which the new Regions and Communities want to emphasise their existence within present-day Belgium, pointing out that the country is not only this but that too.

Belgium as a dream

Apart from some interesting exhibitions on specific topics, two shows in 2005 dealt in some way or another with Belgian history as a whole. The first one, *Made in Belgium*, was set up as a feel-good fancy-fair, showing all sorts of things, fine, wonderful and excellent, that Belgians have accomplished and produced and that have amazed the world. Oh yes, Belgians too have been awarded Nobel Prizes, they have created cartoon figures that became famous all over the globe and their painters and their chocolate and their steel industry surely are the envy of the whole universe. Or at least they should be.

The historic storyline developed through this well-designed exhibition can only be described as absolutely childish, already obsolete a century ago or so. This old-fashioned jingoistic succession of myths, lies, propaganda and make-belief has no connection to any modern critical historiography whatsoever. It thus implicitly declares the historian's work null and void and nobody seems to mind or even to notice. Even the very few comments it provoked raised no further concern, let alone awareness. So much for the status of historiography in Belgium. The show nevertheless became one of the highlights of the celebrations. Even the good King Albert II honoured its opening with his distinguished presence. Although the exhibition was scheduled to close in the fall of 2005, after a few months the decision was made to extend it well into 2006.

On the other hand, there was *Visionary Belgium,* an art show with as its curator the famous Swiss art critic Harald Szeeman, who unfortunately died two weeks before the exhibition opened. As *Made in Belgium* was a one-dimensional collection of simplified national pride, *Visionary Belgium* showed exactly the opposite: an ironic reflection on the soul-searching of the arts in their effort to say something essential on the country, its inhabitants and its history. It pointed out that Belgian art has always been able to express and mirror some fundamental Belgian characteristics, the inability, for instance, to take things too seriously, the consciousness that nothing is what it seems to be, the conviction that earthly urgings are as respectable as idealistic zeal, that humour and poetry are as important as religious fervour or political strife, and the awareness that any idea of one-dimensionality is nothing but a false and pretentious presumption.

In the art of painting this tradition can be traced back from the late nineteenth history, from James Ensor over René Magritte, his fellow surrealists, and Marcel Broodthaers, to present-day artists. Panamarenko imitates life in a purely poetic way by inventing wonderful airplanes that cannot fly and submarines that cannot even float. Wim Delvoye complements poetry with irony and social criticism by building a complicated machine called the *Cloaca.* It really works. It meticulously imitates the human digestive system and indeed produces excrements which, by the way, are on sale for about $1000 apiece, proving that one can indeed sell anything to anybody, as long as the packaging is OK.

For the visitor of *Visionary Belgium* the fun turned out to be far more challenging and sophisticated than the simple joys *Made in Belgium* had on offer. Nevertheless, the two exhibitions have something in common. They both show Belgium as a dream. In spite of its claims to accuracy,

Made in Belgium turns that dream into a populist fantasy history, present-ing myths unbothered by any fact. *Visionary Belgium* explores the other side of the facts, the utopias and other artistic visions they engender. In their own way both shows prove that history is nothing but invention, as indeed the buzzword in international historiography on nation states claims. The exhibitions embody an anarchistic interpretation of reality and history – although it is important to keep in mind that this is not a revolutionary or proletarian anarchism. If it is anything, it should prob-ably be labelled *petit-bourgeois* anarchism, in which mockery is more important than the urge for fundamental change.

Belgium as it grew

B elgium as put on display in 2005 is a dreamt up country, driven by a quixotic ambition to keep the dream alive, to try and overcome division and plurality with a continuous search for compromise and con-sensus. But is Belgium merely a poetic Panamarenko-like work of art that doesn't really work? Or is it a Delvoye-like artificial construction, noth-ing more than a skilfully marketed imitation of reality?

The roots of this conception of the country lay deep in history. The terri-tories that are now part of Belgium for a long time enjoyed relative liberty, based on a well-developed tradition of ancient constitutionalism which guaranteed the local powers (mostly fiscal) freedoms and privileges to which they clung feverously. This tradition gave rise to the development of a vast array of local particularisms, which still persist today. The terri-tories could afford this boastful sense of independence which in the eyes of others might have seemed rather arrogant. But since the Middle Ages, they had the financial means to behave in this way because of the early industrial development of wealthy and thus politically powerful cities and because of the innovative and highly productive agricultural system that sustained them.

Imperialism and expansionism were never prominent characteristics of these territories. They never saw the point in spending a lot of money on the follies of warfare and conquest. Strongly developed local autonomy made it difficult for their lords to collect enough taxes to hire large numbers of mercenaries. Every community wanted to be on its own, to be left alone, minding its own business. Even in the late nineteenth century, King Leopold II observed that Belgians, weary of wasting the taxpayers' money on uncertain adventurism, were immune to the temptations of geopolitical megalomania. So he had to embark on his colonial enterprise on his own.

The territories in the Southern Netherlands never bothered very much with who actually ruled them. For them it was sufficient to make a good deal with their lord, for which their ancient constitutions served as a blueprint. As long as he respected their autonomy and their local privileges, did not interfere with their business, kept taxation on an acceptable level and defended them when their territorial integrity was threatened, they had no problem to be loyal to him. As a result, they also never had the ambition of becoming a military or political power. Even among them relations were far more determined by economic competition than by solidarity or feelings of unity.

Unity was imposed on them from above, as a result of the process of rationalisation and centralisation in the emerging states they were part of. And of course they tried to oppose centralisation as much as they could, if possible by political pressure, if necessary by armed revolt, as happened in the rebellions of the cities against the dukes of Burgundy, the revolt against Spain in the sixteenth century and the uprising against the Habsburg Monarchy in the late eighteenth century.

In the unification process, these territories ended up together, from the seventeenth century onwards in the periphery of the Spanish and Austrian Habsburg empires. Under Spanish rule, they were a Catholic frontline state, on the outskirts of the Counterreformation. When at the beginning of the eighteenth century the centre of power shifted from Madrid to Vienna, they were, well, far away, several times considered only fit to be exchanged for, say, Bavaria, which was a lot closer to the *Hofburg*.

In their relative isolation between a potentially always aggressive France and enemy Protestant countries, the Southern Netherlands were on their own. Ultimately this historic fate transformed their traditional sense of autonomy into a sentiment of national belonging, which was of course a feeling only a political and cultural elite was capable of experiencing. Their annexation by revolutionary France in the 1790s was no pleasant experience at first, but rapidly became an interesting opportunity as France, under pressure of the Continental Blockade, turned out to be a huge market, including Napoleon's armies who needed all those uniforms the Belgian textile industry was happy to provide. By that time, 'Belgium' was already well established as the unofficial name for the Southern Netherlands, indicating the existence of a sense of national identity. It was the result of experiencing a shared history within borders that in essence remained unchanged for two centuries.

The context changed dramatically when the Congress of Vienna, after Napoleon's defeat in Waterloo in 1815, wanted the Dutch King William I to amalgamate the Southern Netherlands with his Northern kingdom. Williams 'United Kingdom' was sapped by mutual distrust from the beginning. As an enlightened despot the King actually wanted to take control of affairs. This was much to the displeasure of the South, as he did not want the Belgians to meddle too much in the affairs of his kingdom, although the Belgian population outweighed the inhabitants in the North two to one. As a Protestant, he wanted to control the Catholic institutions, he also tried to impose Dutch as an official language to the detriment of French which was spoken by the Belgian elites, and he imported a legion of bureaucrats from the North to run things in the South.

This was very different from the kind of 'home rule' the Belgians had become used to. Very soon an opposition developed in the South that led to the formation of the 'monster coalition' between Catholics and Liberals. What these two dominant political tendencies had in a common was their claim to freedom, although the word meant something very different to either of them. The Liberals demanded modern civil liberties and economic freedom. The Catholics wanted to free themselves from royal and state intervention in their affairs, hoping to restore a *de facto* Catholic social order. Like the Liberals, they supported a separation of church and state. After their bad experiences with the Austrians and the French, they gave up the idea of an *Ancien Régime*-like protection of the church by the state and, as most Belgians were Catholics, they counted on the loyalty of the population as a new base for their claims to ideological dominance.

An interesting albeit completely theoretical question might arise here: why did the Liberals of North and South never form an alliance against the absolutist King? The answer probably is: because national bonds were more important than ideological solidarity. The North feared that the Belgians would take control of 'their' kingdom as they were more numerous than the Dutch. It hoped to prevent this by not opposing the despotism of the King, to whom popular representation or proportionality was, of course, as good as irrelevant. With no friends in the North and a potential and eager ally in the South, the choice for the Belgian Liberals was not difficult.

When the Belgian revolution started, a little by accident, after an opera performance in Brussels on August 25, 1830, it was motivated more by mere political frustration than by a genuine project of national independence. The initial claims of the Belgian rebels were very traditional ones: local autonomy and freedom from outside intervention. In a way, they wanted autonomy on the cheap, without having to run a state or pay for it. They wanted things very much to stay as they were and had been for centuries. The fact that Belgium actually gained national independence is not much more than an accident or an irony of history. It simply became unavoidable as every other option proved to be impossible.

Throughout the nineteenth century, Belgium remained very much consensus orientated, a practice which had begun with the 'unnatural' coalition of Catholics and Liberals in 1830 – hence the country's motto "L'union fait la force". If we keep huddling together, no outsider can harm us or disturb our cosy life among ourselves. Strength can only be the result of unity and, as anyone with some experience with human relationships knows, unity is only possible as a result of compromise. In addition, to keep relationships healthy, it is better to forget old quarrels in the past and to cherish the blessings of history.

All this helps to explain Belgium's selective 'official' memory. It should be noted that every nation creates ('invents') its own history with its own myths to justify things as they are. Even the patterns of selection and invention are usually largely the same. The new Belgium saw this as a particularly important task as it thought its survival as a state depended on it. For it took King William nine years to agree to a final separation treaty. Moreover, for decades Belgium felt threatened by the imperialism of its big neighbour France. History had to prove that Belgium had the right to exist.

The theory went that Belgium as a nation could be traced back to Roman times – when Julius Caesar himself called the Belgians "the bravest of the Gauls" [5] – and that since its earliest visible conception under Burgundian rule it had always suffered from invasion, occupation and oppression. The creation of the Belgian state in 1830 was thus presented as the result of a century-long struggle of the Belgians to liberate themselves from Spanish, Austrian, French and Dutch occupation. [6] Here, by the way, the Flemish component of Belgium came in handy: the new state took French culture as its reference, but the Flemish medieval and early modern heritage – the wealthy cities! Rubens! – gave it a particular character that made it fundamentally different from France and thus worthy of independence.

Belgium as it is

A nation-state of course not necessarily equals a democracy. Very early on, an elite had taken control of the revolution. When the constitution was drafted, the right to vote was limited to a tiny minority (less than one percent of the population): the very rich. Suffrage was more restricted than under Dutch rule. Even a number of prominent revolutionaries – especially the journalists, who enjoyed only a moderate income, but had advocated revolutionary change vehemently and idealistically on the public forum – were denied access to political power in the new state. If the original consensus was forged to create a new state, decision-making in its cumbersome first stage of survival could not be weakened by including too many social groups in the process.

To put it more bluntly, the revolution served the Catholic aristocracy of landowners and the rich, mostly Liberal, commercial and industrial bourgeoisie very well. The consensus between those two leading groups intensified as the aristocracy discovered that investing in the fast growing industrial sector proved to be very profitable. At the same time a merchant who had made a fortune in his trade discovered that marrying the daughter of an impoverished nobleman could considerably improve his social status.

This elitist consensus was based on a commonality of interests. The political conflict between Catholics and anticlerical Liberals may have escalated in the course of the nineteenth century, only idiots believed that this was a genuine conflict, as a prominent Catholic statesman once said. Indeed, power shifted to and fro between the emerging Catholic and Liberal parties, but socially the same elite firmly remained in power, representing the same social groups, the landowners and the industrialists. Nevertheless, the original political divide had its significance and illustrates that the ideological fault line cannot be stretched beyond certain limits. In 1857, the Catholics lost power to the Liberals because of their partisan politics favouring exclusively clerical interests. But when a Liberal government 'exaggerated' by attacking those interests, which lead to the first School War (1879-1884), power shifted again to the Catholic party. A consensus always requires moderation.

Soon social protest arose though, not by those who suffered most from inequality, the farmers, but by the industrial labourers. They were better organised and claimed their part of the wealth they helped to bring about in their daily work. The creation of a Socialist movement – which tried to soften its image by omitting any reference to socialism in its original name, the Belgian *Workers'* Party – was instrumental in organising the protest and demanding suffrage extension. Belgium was turned into a country with a very antagonistic class structure. Tensions rose high by the end of the century, ending in violence on both sides. The outbreak of violence marked the limit, making a new consensus necessary.

Around the turn of the century, Belgium was a very paradoxical country. On the one hand, it was one of the economic powerhouses of Europe, the first industrialised nation on the continent and one of the most important exporting countries of the world. On the other hand, it was a country of low wages, with an archaic social system, no social protection at all, generalised poverty and backwardness, with compulsory education and general suffrage (only for men) introduced no earlier than, respectively, 1914 and 1919, with child labour consequently still very common until then.

The growing tensions gave way to the idea of forging a new consensus through the practice of social dialogue. The Belgian Socialists were never tempted by a revolution: in their mainstream they remained reformist, hoping for social reform by taking control of the state through control of parliament. Therefore suffrage had to be extended.

And they found a counterpart in a pragmatic fraction on the other side of the social divide. Those pragmatists were convinced that too much social tension might jeopardise the whole structure of society. And if factory workers are on strike all the time, the factory doesn't produce anything, there is nothing to sell and there are no profits to be made. In some cases, however, bankers secretly gave money to trade unions, so that they could organise strikes as a safety valve, in order to temper unrest and prevent social despair which might provoke the collapse of the whole system. The fraction of the 'enlightened' bankers and industrialists, mostly Liberals, certainly had a hard time convincing the conservative Catholics who controlled the government.

It took a foreign occupation, during World War I, to make a new social consensus possible. The freezing of political life during those four years gave the pragmatists, especially within the monopolistic holding *Société Générale*, which controlled most of Belgium's (and later Congo's) industrial and financial system, the opportunity to create a *fait accompli* by deciding that the granting of the general suffrage and the introduction of several social laws were inevitable. They also possessed a forum for discussion: the committee that organised the provision of occupied Belgium with goods supplied by charities abroad.[7] They mapped out a new future for the country and got the approval of King Albert, who was probably the most pragmatic of them all. It is no coincidence that more than half of the ministers in the first post-war government were former members of the committee. In order to assure social peace and stability the Socialists were included in the parliamentary system.

Of course, there was a risk. Now the left – the Socialists and the progressive Christian-Democrats – theoretically could take control of government. The economic and financial elite avoided this by organising a social dialogue outside the traditional political system. Together with the trade unions, which wanted direct access to power, they denied Parliament any control over economic and social issues by entrusting those to a separate forum of discussion. There the industrialists and the trade unions negotiated as equals. Among them the balance of power was not influenced by electoral results but by bargaining skills. And as a result of the rivalry between the Socialist and Christian-Democrat trade unions, big business mostly ended up as the winner. Only the bill – e.g., for financing social benefits – was sent to Parliament for formal approval and execution. A new consensus came about; it laid the foundations for the welfare state that emerged after Word War II.

The limits of consensus

Only once this consensus was compromised: during the Royal Question. The Catholic party, which still firmly controlled the Flemish part of the country, tried to gamble. Thinking the monarchy popular enough to withstand the criticism against King Leopold III, it allied itself fully with the royal cause. It hoped that through the popularity of the King it would win an absolute majority in parliament, by which it could impose the supremacy of Catholic conservatism on the whole of the country. This meant a major break in a by then firmly rooted political tradition of consensus, compromise and power sharing between all the major players in the field. The probably exaggerated threat of a civil war made the Catholics realise that they could not rule against the will of a significant minority, in this case of Walloons and Socialists. Discreet talks between party leaders – not an open discussion in Parliament – lead to a restoration of consensus. The struggle ended in 1950 with the defeat of the Catholic radicals, symbolised by the abdication of the King whom they had chosen as their figurehead.

A few years later, a potentially similar conflict arose when from 1954 on, a coalition of Socialists and Liberals tried to promote state education at the expense of the vast Catholic school system. Lacking a parliamentary majority, the Catholic 'pillar' – the complex system of Catholic associations – reacted by organising massive protest marches in Brussels. After this show of force the so-called second School War did not end in Parliament either but, again, in a separate negotiation. Only the conclusion was shown publicly: the signing of a formal School Pact in 1958. Its name echoed the Social Pact of 1944, by which the so-called social partners had decided to continue and reinforce the pre-war tradition of social negotiations as a way of organising labour relations. In the early 1970s, a Culture Pact was signed, which set the rules of the ideological game and made sure that no ideological or philosophical minority was to suffer discrimination.

The Royal Question and the School War show a similar pattern. A legitimate political majority makes a political decision which threatens a vital interest of the opposition and thus breaks the consensus. The latter is restored after some kind of collective action in the streets, the alternative to parliamentary action, that forces the majority to reconsider its earlier decision. Then a compromise is made – and the conflict soon forgotten.

The tradition has proven its use, but there is a disadvantage to it too. It depends on a permanent, bargaining-skilled elite, which limits real insight, participation and power to a handful of people, who conduct their business outside the public's view. Confidentiality is of the essence, which does not contribute to the democratic transparency of the political system nor to any real involvement of the public opinion. It often keeps essential information out of the reach of journalists and, later on, of historians.

For more than a century, the gatekeepers easily succeeded in managing this system. Nowadays, however, the sustainability of the practice seems far more questionable as the lack of transparency has entailed a widespread public distrust of the political institutions and of the elites who run them. The electoral success of populist and right-wing extremism is an expression of these fundamental public doubts. Yet the culture of consensus has brought about a fundamental sense of moderation and compromise. The willingness to enter into structural negotiations and to avoid a 'majority dictatorship' is probably the main reason why violence, bloodshed and terrorism are absent from Belgium's political history, especially in the twentieth century.

But although the long tradition of consensus has guaranteed Belgium's political stability and relative peacefulness, it has its limits. First, it should be noted that a compromise is essentially a practical and pragmatic solution, not an idealistic state of mind. The culture of consensus did not prevent Belgians from living separated from others with different opinions and convictions for a long time. Class segregation is a well-known phenomenon in Belgium too. The development of the ideological 'pillars' – a Catholic, a Socialist, a small Liberal and a Flemish-nationalist pillar which is even tinier – meant that each group lived in an isolated sphere, with its own schools, trade-unions, newspapers, women's and youth organisations, health services, shops, (film) theatres, sports clubs, brass bands etc. Only commercialisation and privatisation could put an end to this structural segregation. But for a long time, a Socialist, say, could spend his whole life without ever having to talk to a Catholic. In a way, Belgium was not a society but a conglomeration of societies.

Second, the tradition of consensus does not seem effective as far as linguistic division is concerned. As a result of the waning of the old 'national' elite and the growing dissimilarities within the country, it started a long process of constitutional reform from 1970 onwards in order to overcome the conflicts between Flemings and Francophones. Every new phase claims to be the last but devolution nevertheless keeps dragging on, as if every new step brings about the need for a further deepening of federalism. That is probably the way it works: a compromise is never enough. It seems impossible to settle the matter once and for all.

In the end, only separation – i.e., the unwillingness to compromise any more – seems the only final solution to the problem. This has been done before, as the pillars have proven at the time they were still almighty. The difference is that linguistic separation is linked to territories. Members of different pillars lived in the same streets and in the same towns. Linguistic groups essentially live between territorial borders, geographically isolating them from the others, Brussels being the only – although numerically and symbolically very important – exception. Culturally this separation is already a fact, as Dutch and French speakers no longer share any significant common medium of communication. They do not read each other's papers anymore, they do not watch each other's television programmes, they do not have the same role models. This makes the end of Belgium as a state a conceivable option in a not too distant future. But whether this will be the result of a self-fulfilling prophecy or of the genuine wish of the Belgians still remains to be seen.

As it happens, opinion polls indicate that loyalty to Belgian unity is still widespread and dominant all over the country. Maybe the idea that Belgium is nearing its end as a viable state is only a myopic or post-modern interpretation of the Belgian people's eternal inclination to localism.

1   This attention was solely generated by the success of the Flemish film *Daens* (1992), a biopic directed by Stijn Coninx, on the life of the priest who led the Daensist movement. In the year of its release, the film was nominated for an Oscar in the category Foreign Language Films.

2   www.diplobel.org/uk/pages/news/newsletters/LeopoldII.doc.
    It is interesting to note that the Belgian government did not react to books published earlier (and which were translated in Dutch en French) which made similar allegations (e.g., Adam Hochschild, *King Leopold's Ghosts. A story of greed, terror and heroism in Colonial Africa*, New York, 1998).

3   A notable defender of the King was his friend Roger Keyes, who published a book on the matter, which was also translated in Dutch and French: *Outrageous Fortune. The tragedy of Leopold III of the Belgians 1901-1941* (London, 1984).

4   Ludo De Witte, *The Assassination of Lumumba* (London, 2001 – original Dutch publication: 1999).

5   In fact, the 'Belgae' Caesar wrote about (in his *De bello gallico*) were a people that largely lived in the Northern part of today's France.

6   Historians may know this theory to be proven wrong, it nevertheless is still very popular today. The exhibition *Made in Belgium* mentioned above uses it as a guiding idea, stretching the concept of invasion to the German occupation of Belgium in both World Wars. The idea implies that Belgians never had legitimate rulers, which explains their distrust for the state, their inability to recognise or obey authorities, their soft anarchism, their tendency to evade taxes, their lack of social discipline, even their inclination to disregard speed limits. Flemish nationalists have 'modernised' the theory by applying it to Flanders, thus including Belgium in the list of 'foreign' (i.e., French speaking) oppressors. For those separatists, liberation is still to come and will be achieved by the creation of an independent Flemish state.

7   As both World Wars proved, politicians who do not flee the country when it is invaded, turn out to be the most influential ones once the war is over. Being able to stay in touch with the mood of the country is probably the salient factor. In 1940, when the country was invaded again, the government tried to avoid the concentration of *de facto* power in a new committee-like political forum, by splitting authority between the top civil servants, whom it put in charge of the Belgium's bureaucracy, and the so-called *Comité Galopin*, consisting of bankers, that was asked to take care of economic and financial matters.

Selected Bibliography

The following selection is by no means exhaustive. The main idea is to suggest further (relatively) recent literature in English on the diverse aspects of Belgium which were treated above, in addition to some others which unfortunately were not.

War

Barton, Peter, Peter Doyle & Johan Vandewalle. *Beneath Flanders Fields. The tunnellers' war 1914-1918*. Staplehurst: Spellmount, 2005.

Evans, Martin Marnix. *Passchendaele and the Battles of Ypres 1914-1918*. London: Osprey Military, 1997.

Harrison, R.T. *The German Occupation of Belgium 1914-1918*. Stafford: J.B. Horne, 1986.

Horne, John & Alan Kramer. *German Atrocities, 1914. A history of denial*, New Haven, CN/London: Yale University Press, 2001.

Johansson, Rune. *Small State in Boundary Conflict. Belgium and the Belgian-German border, 1914-1919*. Lund (*Studies in International History*, 24), 1988.

MacDonald, Lyn. *They called it Passchendaele. The story of the Third Battle of Ypres and of the men who fought in it*. London: MacMillan, 1983.

Marks, Sally. *Innocent Abroad. Belgium at the Paris Peace Conference of 1919*. Chapel Hill, NC: University of North Carolina Press, 1981.

Schaepdrijver, Sophie, de. 'Death Is Elsewhere: The Shifting Locus of Tragedy in Belgian First World War Literature'. *Yale French Studies*, Theme Issue 102: *Belgian Memories*, Catherine Labio ed., 2002, 94-114.

Schaepdrijver, Sophie, de. 'Occupation, Propaganda, and the Idea of Belgium'. In Aviel Roshwald & Richard Stites (Eds). *European Culture in the Great War. The arts, entertainment, and propaganda, 1914-1918*. Cambridge: Cambridge University Press, 1999, 267-294.

Wolff, Leon. *In Flanders Fields. The 1917 campaign*. London: The Folio Society, 2003.

Zuckerman, Larry. *The Rape of Belgium. The untold story of World War I*. New York/London: New York University Press, 2004.

Belgium, September 1944. An Anglo-Belgian symposium to commemorate the fortieth anniversary of the liberation of Belgium. London, The Imperial War Museum, August 21-22, 1984. Brussels: Ministry of Foreign Affairs, External Trade and Cooperation in Development, 1985 (Memo from Belgium. Views and Surveys, Vol. 195).

Conway, Martin. *Collaboration in Belgium. Léon Degrelle and the Rexist Movement 1940-1944*. New Haven, CN/London: Yale University Press, 1993.

Belgian Forces in United Kingdom. Brussels: Fédération des anciens combatants de la Brigade Piron, 1994.

Lagrou, Pieter. *The Legacy of Nazi Occupation. Patriotic memory and national recovery in Western Europe, 1945-1965*. Cambridge: Cambridge University Press, 2000.

Man, Paul, De (Werner Hamacher ed.). *Wartime Journalism, 1939-1943*. Lincoln, NE/London: University of Nebraska Press, 1988.

Michman, Dan, ed. *Belgium and the Holocaust. Jews, Belgians and Germans*. Jerusalem: Yad Vashem, 1998.

Warmbrunn, Werner. *The German Occupation of Belgium 1940-1944*. Bern/New York/Paris: Peter Lang, 1993.

Language

Craen, P. Van de & R. Willemyns. 'The Standardization of Dutch in Flanders'. *International Journal of Sociology of Language 73* (1988), 45-64.

Deprez, Kas, ed. *Language and Intergroup Relations in Flanders and the Netherlands.* Dordrecht: Foris, 1989.

Donaldson, Bruce C. *Dutch. A linguistic history of Holland and Belgium.* Leiden: Nijhoff, 1983.

Durme, L. van. 'Genesis and Evolution of the Romance-Germanic Language Border in Europe'. In Jeanine Caroline Treffers-Daller & Roland Willemyns (Eds). *Language Contact at the Romance-Germanic Language Border.* Clevedon: Multilingual Matters, 2002 (*Journal of multilingual and multicultural development*, 23, 1-2), 9-21.

Hout, Roeland, Van & Uus Knops (Eds). *Language attitudes in the Dutch Language Area.* Dordrecht: Foris, 1988.

Murphy, Alexander B. *The Regional Dynamics of Language Differentiation in Belgium. A study in cultural-political geography.* Chicago, IL: University of Chicago, 1988.

O'Neill, Michael. 'Language, Ethnicity and Nationality in Belgium'. In Michael O'Neill & Dennis Austin (Eds). *Democracy and Cultural Diversity.* Oxford: University Press, 2000.

Treffers-Daller, Jeanine Caroline. 'Language Use and Language Contact in Brussels'. In Jeanine Caroline Treffers-Daller & Roland Willemyns, eds. *Language Contact at the Romance-Germanic Language Border.* Clevedon: Multilingual Matters, 2002 (*Journal of multilingual and multicultural development*, 23, 1-2), 50-64.

Vandeputte, Omer. *Dutch. The language of twenty million Dutch and Flemish people.* Rekkem: Stichting Ons Erfdeel, 1981.

Verdoodt, Albert. *Sociology of Language in Belgium.* Berlin/New York: M. de Gruyter, 1993.

Willemyns, R. 'Dutch in the European Union: The Language Policy of the 'Nederlandse Taalunie". *Sociolinguistica XI* (1997), 53-62.

Witte, Els & Harry Van Velthoven. *Language and Politics. The Belgian case study in a historical perspective.* Brussels: VUBPress, 1999.

Witte, Els & Hugo Baetens Beardsmore (Eds). *The Interdisciplinary Study of Urban Bilingualism in Brussels,* Clevedon: Multilingual Matters, 1987.

Wright, Sue & Hellen Kelly (Eds). *Language in Contact and Conflict. Contrasting experiences in the Netherlands and Belgium.* Clevedon: Multilingual Matters, 1995.

Consensus

Alen, André. *Belgium. Bipolar and centrifugal federalism,* Brussels: Ministry for Foreign Affairs, 1990.

Alen, André, Rusen Ergec e.a. *Federal Belgium after the Fourth State Reform of 1993.* Brussels: Ministry of Foreign Affairs, External Trade and Development Cooperation, 2nd ed., 1998.

Bodson, Philippe, Etienne Davignon e.a. *Belgium. Unity of diversity.* Tielt: Lannoo, 1987.

The Belgian Constitution. Brussels: Parliament. The Belgian House of Representatives, 2002.

D'Haenens, Albert. *150 Years of Communities and Cultures in Belgium 1830-1990.* Brussels: Ministry of Foreign Affairs, 1980.

Fitzmaurice, John. *The Politics of Belgium. A unique federalism,* Boulder, CO/ London: Westview Press, 1996.

The Institutions of Federal Belgium. An introduction to Belgian public law. Leuven: Acco, 2nd ed., 2001.

Lijphart, Arend (Ed). *Conflict and Coexistence in Belgium. The dynamics of a culturally divided society.* Berkeley, CA: Institute of International Studies, University of Berkeley, 1981.

Martiniello, Marco (Ed). *Multicultural Policies and the State. A comparison of two European societies.* Utrecht: European Research Centre on Migration and Ethnic Relations, Utrecht University, 1998.

Mc Rae, K. *Conflict and Compromise in Multilingual Societies. Belgium.* Waterloo, ON: Wilgrid Laurier University Press, 1986.

Timmermans, Arco I. *High Politics in the Low Countries. An empirical study of coalition agreements in Belgium and the Netherlands.* Ashgate: Aldershot, 2003.

Warden, J.G. *Belgium, Management of the Community Crisis 1961-1981.* Leicester: University of Leicester, 1985.

History & Politics

Ascherson, Neal. *The King Incorporated. Leopold the Second and the Congo.* (Allen & Unwin, 1963) London: Granta, 1999, new ed.

Blom, J.C.H. & E. Lambrechts (Eds). *History of the Low Countries.* New York: Berghahn Books, 1999.

Caestecker, Frank. *Alien Policy in Belgium, 1840-1940. The creation of guest workers, refugees and illegal aliens.* New York/Oxford: Berghahn Books, 2000.

Cook, Bernard A. *Belgium. A history.* New York/Bern/Brussels: Peter Lang, 2004.

Deprez, Kas & Louis Vos (Eds). *Nationalism in Belgium. Shifting identities, 1780-1995.* Basingstoke: Macmillan, 1998.

Ewans, Martin. *European Atrocity, African Catastrophe. Leopold II, the Congo Free State and its aftermath.* London/New York: Routledge Curzon, 2002.

Hermans, Theo, Louis Vos & Lode Wils (Eds). *The Flemish Movement. A documentary history, 1780-1990.* Atlantic Highlands, JN: Athlone Press, 1992.

Hilden, Patricia. *Women, Work and Politics: Belgium, 1830-1914.* Oxford: Clarendon Press, 1993.

Hochschild, Adam. *King Leopold's Ghost. A story of greed, terror and heroism in Colonial Africa*. Boston, MA: Houghton Mifflin, 1998.

Keyes, Roger. *Outrageous Fortune. The tragedy of Leopold III of the Belgians, 1901-1941*. London: Secker and Warburg, 1984.

Kossmann, E. H. *The Low Countries*. Oxford: Oxford University Press, 1978.

Lyon, Bruce. *Henri Pirenne. A biography and intellectual study*. Gent: E. Story-Scientia, 1974.

Murray, John J. *Flanders & England: a Cultural Bridge. The influence of the Low Countries on Tudor-Stuart England*. Antwerpen: Mercator, 1985.

Robin, L. Hogg. *Structural Rigidities and Policy Inertia in Inter-War Belgium*. Brussel: KVAB, 1986 (Verhandelingen, Klasse der Letteren, no. 118).

Rooney, John W. *Revolt in the Netherlands. Brussels 1830*. Lawrence, KS: Coronado Press, 1982.

Rudd, C. *An Historical and Empirical Analysis of the Belgian Party System. National and sub-national perspectives*. Colchester: University of Essex, 1986.

Rynck, Stefaan, De. *Changing Public Policy. The role of the regions: educational and environmental policy in Belgium*. Brussels/New York: Peter Lang, 2002.

Strikwerda, Carl. *A House Divided. Catholics, socialists and Flemish nationalists in nineteenth-century Belgium*. Lanham/Boulder/New York/London: Rowman & Littlefield, 1997.

Vos-Hughes, Antoinette, De. *Family Life of the Belgian Bourgeoisie in the Interwar Period*. Milton Keynes: Open University, 2001.

Walgrave, Stefaan e.a. *Ministerial Cabinets and Partitocracy. A career pattern study of ministerial cabinet members in Belgium*. Antwerpen: Universiteit Antwerpen, 2004.

Witte, Els, Jan Craeybeckx & Alain Meynen. *Political History of Belgium from 1830 onwards*. Brussel/Antwerpen: Standaard, 2000.

Witte, Ludo, de. *The Assassination of Lumumba*. London: Verso, 2001.

Zolberg, A.R. 'The Making of Flemings and Walloons: Belgium 1830-1914'. *Journal of Interdisciplinary History*, 5 (1974), 179-234.

Economics

Blomme, Jan. *The Economic Development of Belgian Agriculture in 1880-1980. A quantitative and qualitative analysis*. Leuven: Leuven University Press, 1993.

Higginson, John. *A Working Class in the Making. Belgian colonial labor policy, private enterprise, and the African mineworker, 1907-1951*. Madison, WI: University of Wisconsin Press, 1989.

Mokyr, Joel. *Industrialization in the Low Countries, 1795-1850*. New Haven, CN: Yale University Press, 1976.

Mommen, André. *The Belgian Economy in the Twentieth Century*. London: Routledge, 1994.

Wee, Herman, Van der & Jan Blomme. *The Economic Development of Belgium since 1870*. Cheltenham: Elgar, 1997.

The Arts

The Low Countries. Arts and society in Flanders and the Netherlands. Rekkem: Stichting Ons Erfdeel – appears annually since 1993.

Bekaert, Geert. *Contemporary Architecture in Belgium*. Tielt: Lannoo, 1995.

Claus, Hugo. *The Sorrow of Belgium*. Harmondsworth: Penguin, 1991.

Derycke, Luc & Sandra Van De Veire (Eds). *Belgian Fashion Design*. Gent: Ludion, 1999.

Delvaux, André & Marianne Thys. *Belgian Cinema / Le cinéma belge/ De Belgische film*. Brussel: Koninklijk Belgisch Filmarchief – Gent /Amsterdam: Ludion, 1999.

Dierkens-Aubry, Françoise. *Art Nouveau in Belgium. Architecture & interior design*. Tielt: Lannoo, 1996.

International Theatre Institute. *The Theatre in French-speaking Belgium since 1945*. Brussels: Archives et Musée de la Littérature, 1991.

Linkhorn, Renée & Judy Cochran (Eds). *Belgian Women Poets. An anthology*. New York/Frankfurt am Main/Brussels: Peter Lang, 2000.

Loze, Pierre. *Belgium Art Nouveau. From Victor Horta to Antoine Pompe*. Gent: Snoeck-Ducaju, 1991.

Palmer, Michael. *From Ensor to Magritte. Belgian art, 1880-1940*. Brussels: Racine, 1994.

Peeters, Benoît. *Tintin and the World of Hergé*. London: Methuen Children's, 1989.

Roberts-Jones, Philippe. *The History of Painting in Belgium, from the 14th century to the present day, from the earliest masters of the old southern Netherlands and the principality of Liège to our contemporary artists*. Brussels: La Renaissance du Livre, 1995.

Screech, Matthew. *Masters of the Ninth Art. Bandes dessinées and Franco-Belgian identity*. Liverpool: Liverpool University Press, 2005.

Cities

Burke, Peter. *Antwerp: a metropolis in comparative perspective*. Gent: Snoeck-Ducaju, 1993.

Derez, Mark. *Leuven: town and gown*. Tielt: Lannoo, 1991.

Decavele, Johan. *Gent: historisch hart van Vlaanderen – historical heart of Flanders*. Gent: Snoeck-Ducaju, 1985.

Isacker, Karel, Van & Raymond van Uytven. *Antwerp: twelve centuries of history and culture*. Antwerpen: Mercator, 1986.

Murray, James. *Bruges. The cradle of capitalism, 1280-1390*. Cambridge: Cambridge University Press, 2005.

Roberts-Jones, Philippe (Ed). *Brussels Fin de Siècle*. Köln/London: Taschen, 1999.

Miscellaneous

Boudart, Marina & Boudart Michel (Eds). *Modern Belgium*. Palo Alto, CA: Society for the Promotion of Science and Scholarship, 1990.

Bryssinck René (Ed). *Modern Belgium*. Brussels: Modern Belgium Association, 1990.

Carson, Patricia. *The Fair Face of Flanders*. Tielt: Lannoo, 1995.

Eppink, Derk-Jan. *Belgian Adventures. A European discovers Belgium*. Tielt: Lannoo, 2004.

Fox, Renée C. *In the Belgian Château. The spirit and culture of a European society in an age of change*. Chicago: Ivan R. Dee, 1994.

Frommer, Arthur. *A Masterpiece Called Belgium*. New York: Prentice Hall, 1989.

Goscinny & Uderzo. *Asterix in Belgium*. London: Hodder Dargaud, 1980.

Harvey, R. Graham. *The Belgian National Song 'La Brabançonne' arranged & adapted to English words*. London: F. Pitman Hart & Co, s.d.

Lacy, M.B. (Ed). *The Low Countries. Multidisciplinary studies*. Lanham, MD: University Press of America, 1990.

Mouton, Olivier, Marie-Anne Wilssens, Frédéric Antoine, Marc Reynebeau. *Belgium. A state of mind*, Tielt: Lannoo, 2001.

Sante, Luc. *The Factory of Facts*. New York/London: Pantheon/Granta, 1998.

Notes on the Contributors

Benno Barnard was born in Amsterdam in 1954, and moved to Brussels as a young grown-up. Primarily an author of poetry, essays and theatre plays, Barnard has also published extensively on Belgian issues, regarding his host country as a relevant scale model for European integration. His most important book on European history is *Eeuwrest* (Rest of the Century, Atlas, 2001).

Martine Van Berlo has been lector for Dutch in the Department of Germanic Studies, Trinity College Dublin (Ireland) since 2004.

After studying Dutch and German language and literature at the University of Antwerp she taught Dutch in Belgium, the Netherlands, France, and for seven years at universities in Germany.

Berlo coordinated the translation of Benno Barnard's *Europa's Bastard* into German (Eupen, 2000) and published a history of the Dutch lectorate at the University of Freiburg (Germany) in the *Festschrift Heinrich Anz* (Freiburg 2002).

She organised the Symposium *Belgium Revealed*, on 175 years of Belgian independence, at Trinity College Dublin (April 2005).

Geert van Istendael studied sociology and philosophy at the University of Leuven and embarked for some time on a research career. Between 1978 and 1993 he worked as a journalist for the Belgian public television news (VRT, Dutch language), specialising in Belgian politics, urban and community problems in Brussels, and Germany.

From 1993 on, Istendael works as an independent writer based in Brussels. He has published a number of essays, three collections of poetry and two novels and makes regular contributions to Dutch and Belgian radio, newspapers and weeklies. He has also translated poetry and theatre into Dutch, e.g. Brecht, Brel, Fried, Goethe, Heine, Kahlau and Yeats. He is the co-president (together with Marion Hansel) of *Kunstenfestival DesArts* in Brussels.

In his book *Het Belgisch labyrint* (The Belgian Labyrinth, De Arbeiderspers, 1989, 16th edition 2005) Istendael tries to explain the intricacies and delicacies of his fatherland to foreigners. It is translated into French, Hungarian and Czech.

Tony Judt was educated at King's College, Cambridge and the *Ecole Normale Supérieure*, Paris. He has taught at Cambridge, Oxford, Berkeley and New York University, where he is currently the Erich Maria Remarque Professor of European Studies and Director of the Remarque Institute, which he founded in 1995. He is Fellow of the Royal Historical Society and of the American Academy of Arts and Sciences.

Judt is the author or editor of twelve books, mostly on modern European history and the history of ideas. He is also a frequent contributor to the *New York Review of Books*, the *Times Literary Supplement*, *The New Republic*, *The New York Times* and many other journals in Europe and the US.

His new book, *Postwar. A history of Europe since 1945*, will be published by Penguin in 2005.

Marc Reynebeau works as an editor and columnist for the Flemish quality paper *De Standaard*.

As an independent and critical historian, he has published extensively on the Flemish Movement (e.g., *Het klauwen van de leeuw* – The Clawing of the

Lion, Van Halewijck, 1995) and on Belgian history (e.g., *Een geschiedenis van België* – A history of Belgium, Lannoo, 2003; a French edition will be published in 2005).

Reynebeau is often asked to comment on (historically) sensitive political issues and frequently tries to bridge the cultural 'gap' by explaining the 'Flemish' perspective in the French-speaking media.

He also publishes cultural and literary criticism and is a respected expert on Paul van Ostaijen, the first Flemish modernist poet (1896-1928).

Sophie de Schaepdrijver studied history in Brussels, Florence, and Amsterdam, where she obtained her Ph.D. in 1990 with the monograph *Elites for the Capital? Foreign Migration to Mid-Nineteenth Century Brussels* (Thesis Publishers, 1990). Her second book, *De Groote Oorlog: het Koninkrijk België tijdens de Eerste Wereldoorlog* (The Kingdom of Belgium in the First World War, Atlas, 1997), was awarded the 1999 Flemish Free Speech Prize (*Arkprijs van het Vrije Woord*) for its approach to issues of collaboration. An updated French translation has appeared under the title *La Belgique et la Première Guerre Mondiale* (P.I.E./Peter Lang, 2004).

Living in the United States since 1995, Schaepdrijver held a fellowship at the national Humanities Center and taught at New York University. Now Associate Professor of Modern European History at The Pennsylvania State University, she is preparing a study (in English) on Belgium's '14-'18 experience of military occupation and its aftermath.

She has also contributed columns and essays to the Belgian press, published under the title *Taferelen uit het burgerleven: Essays en Aantekeningen* (Scenes From Bourgeois Life: Essays and Notes, Atlas, 2002).